ABC's & 123's
of Abstract
Kids & Adults De-Stress
Coloring Book

Benjamin Allen

DEDICATION

This book is dedicated to all who are young at heart.
You are never too young, or to old, to enjoy your ABC's & 123's.

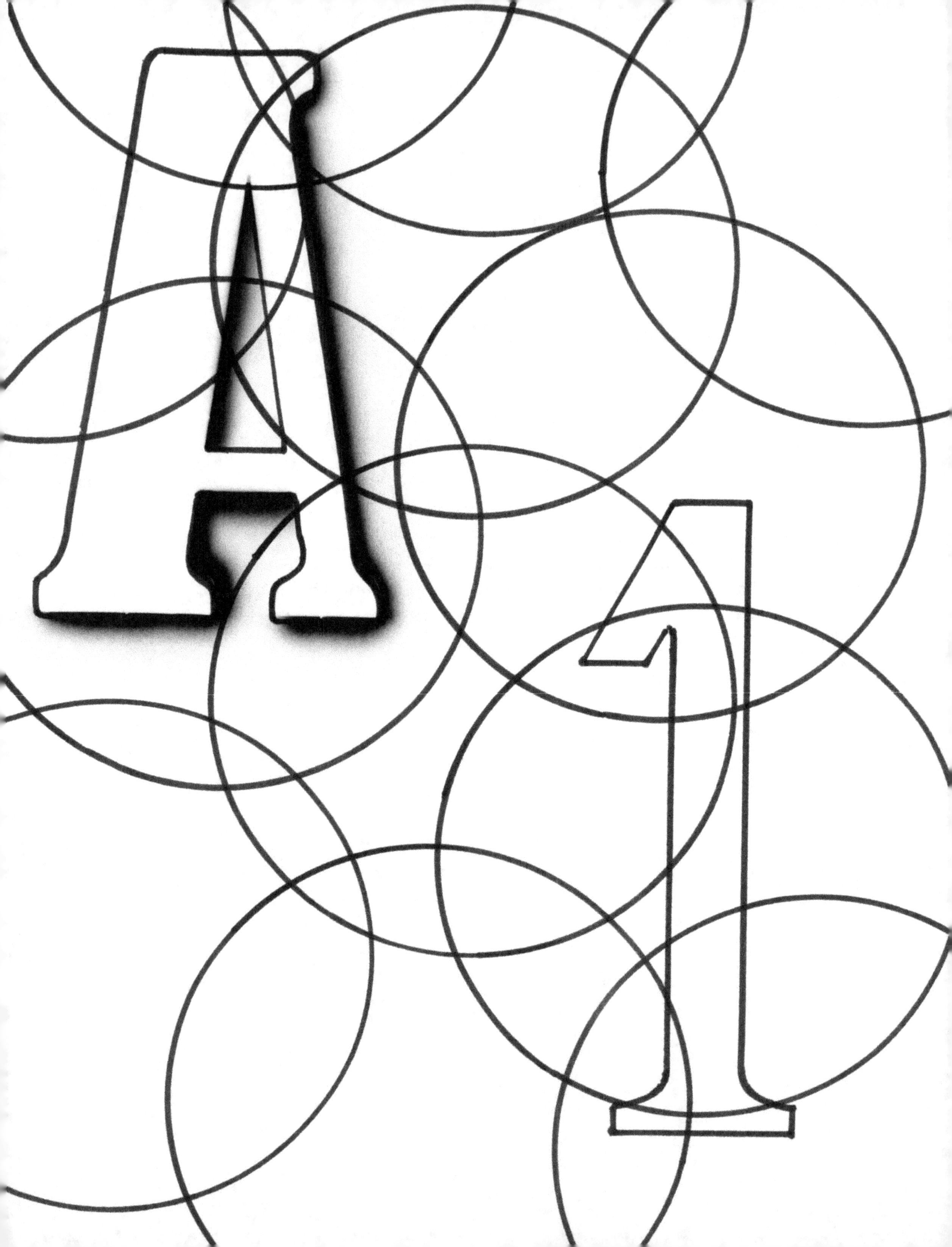

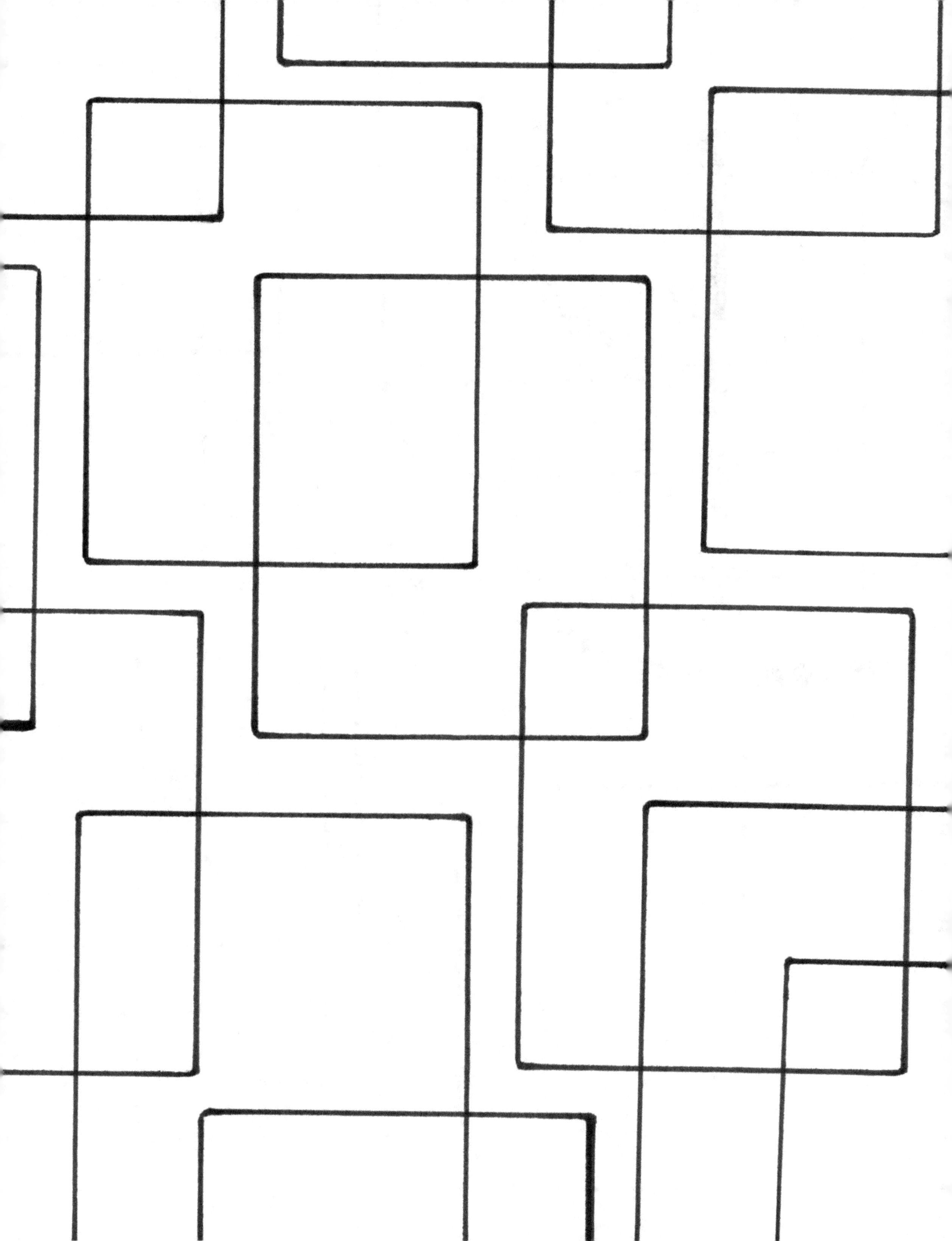

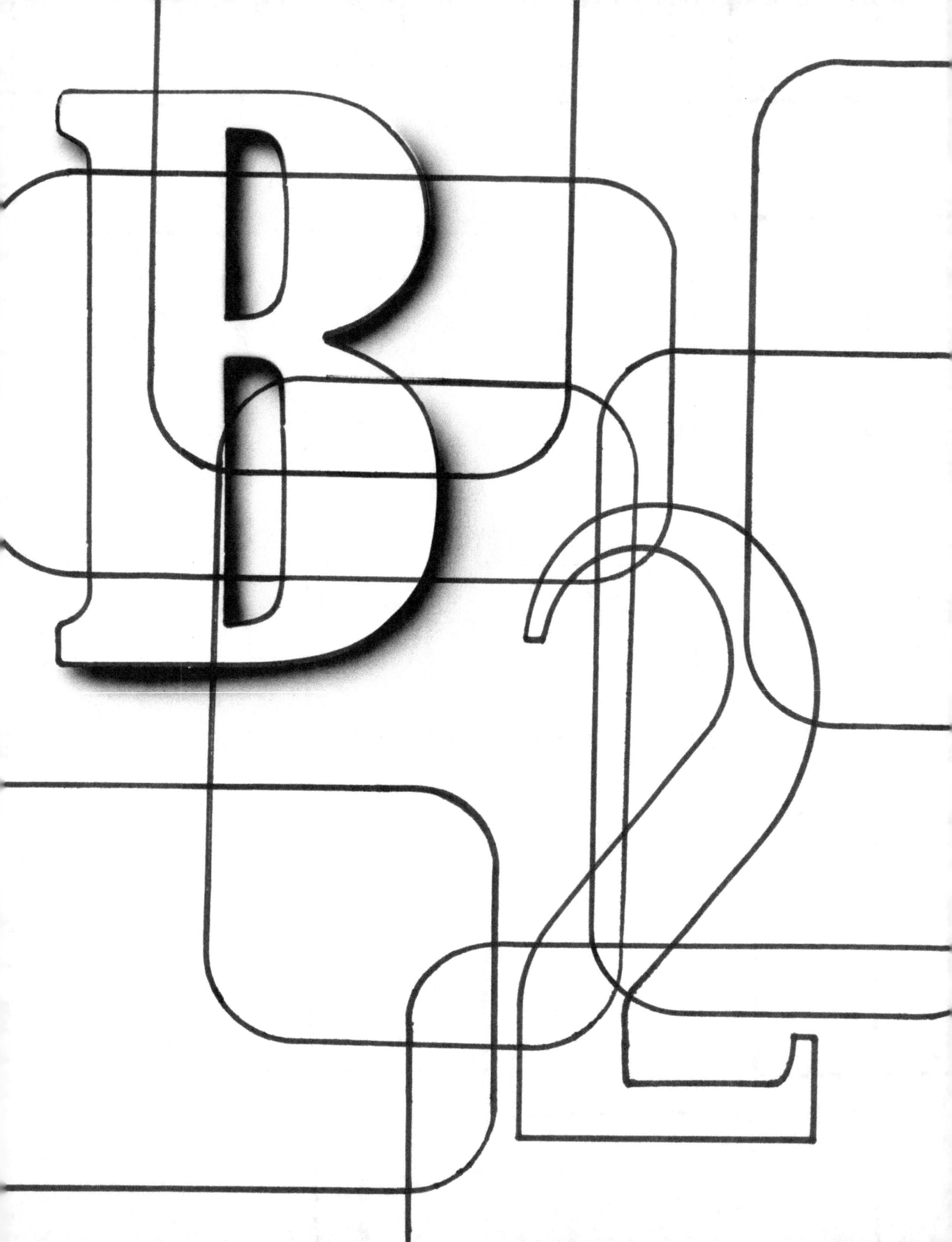

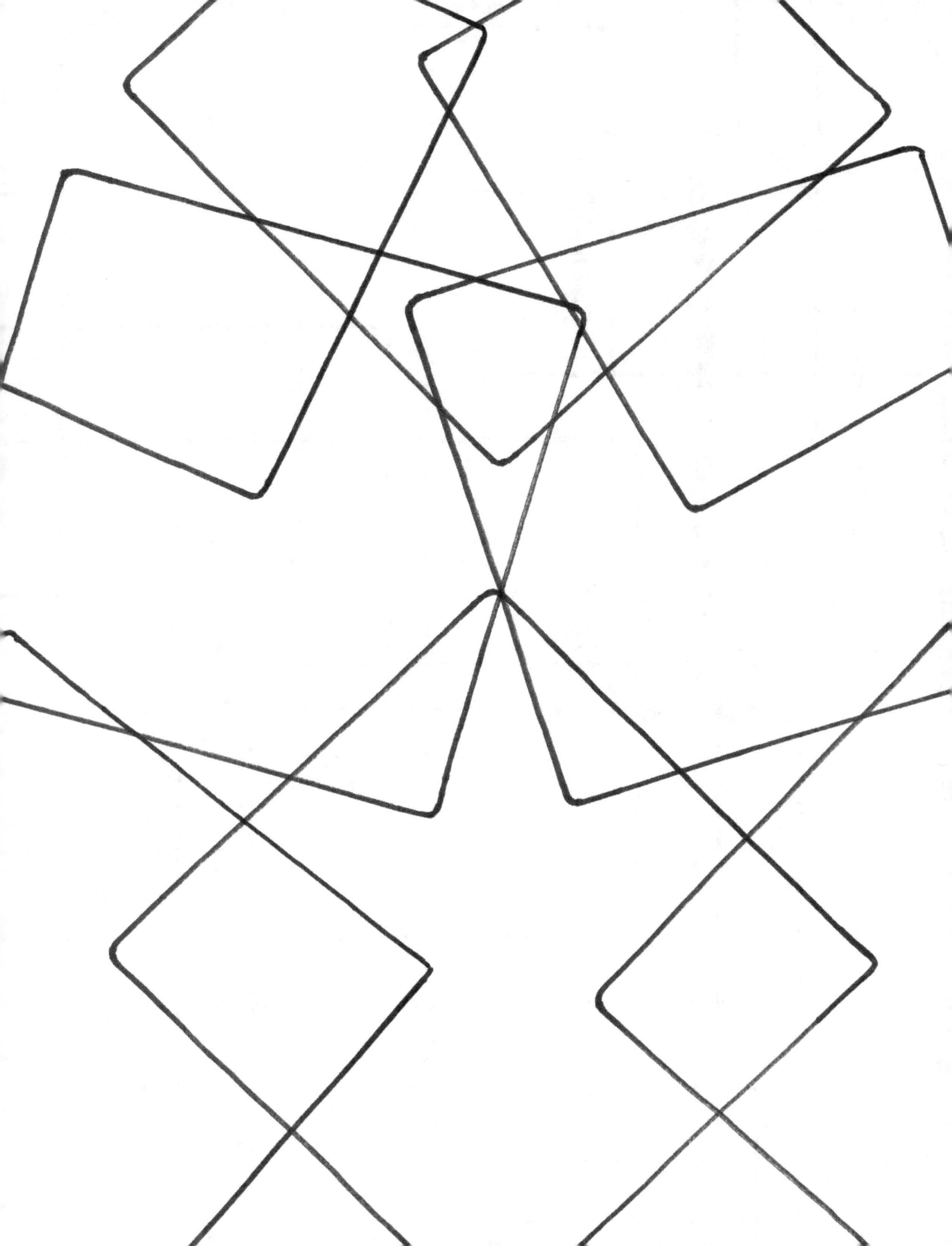

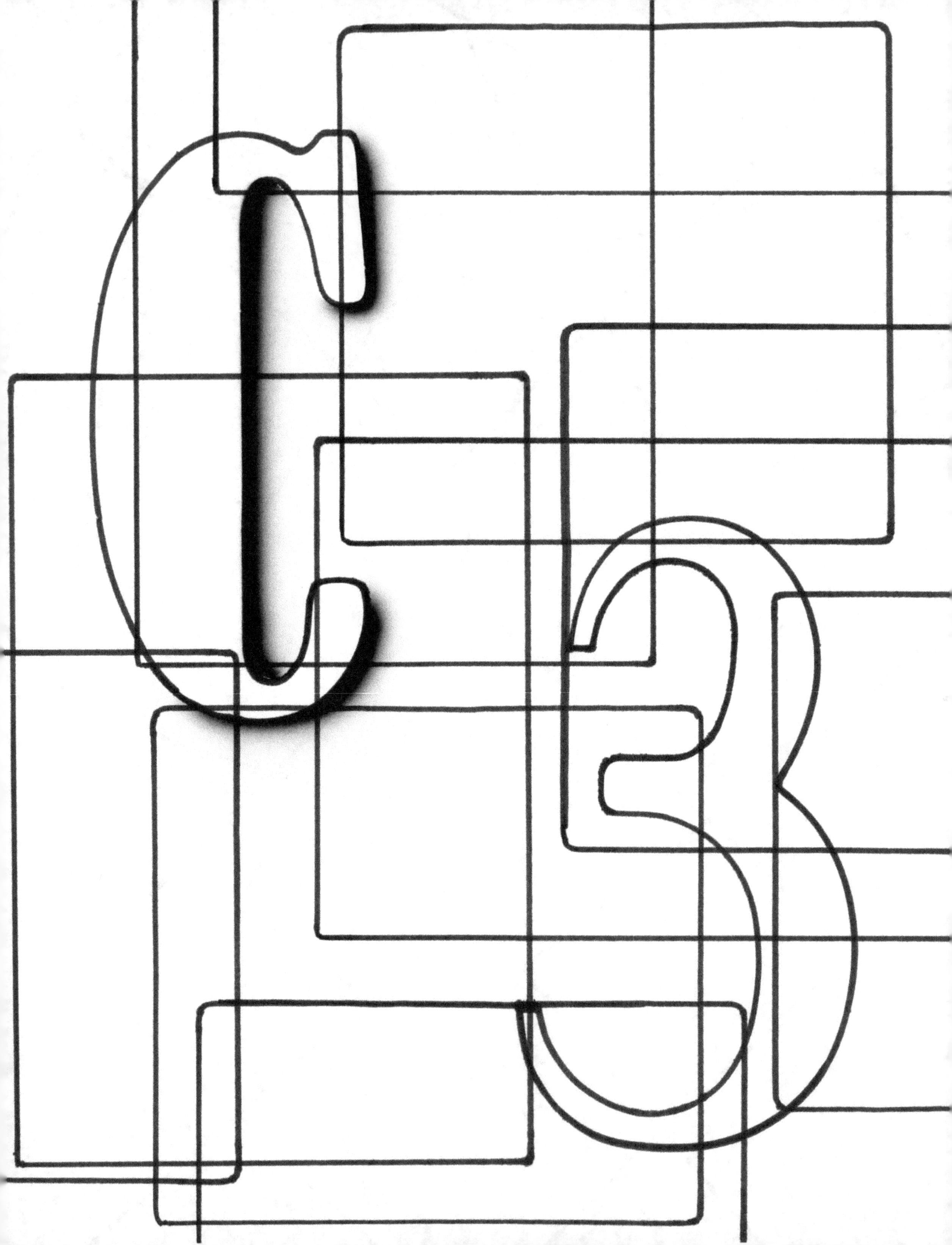

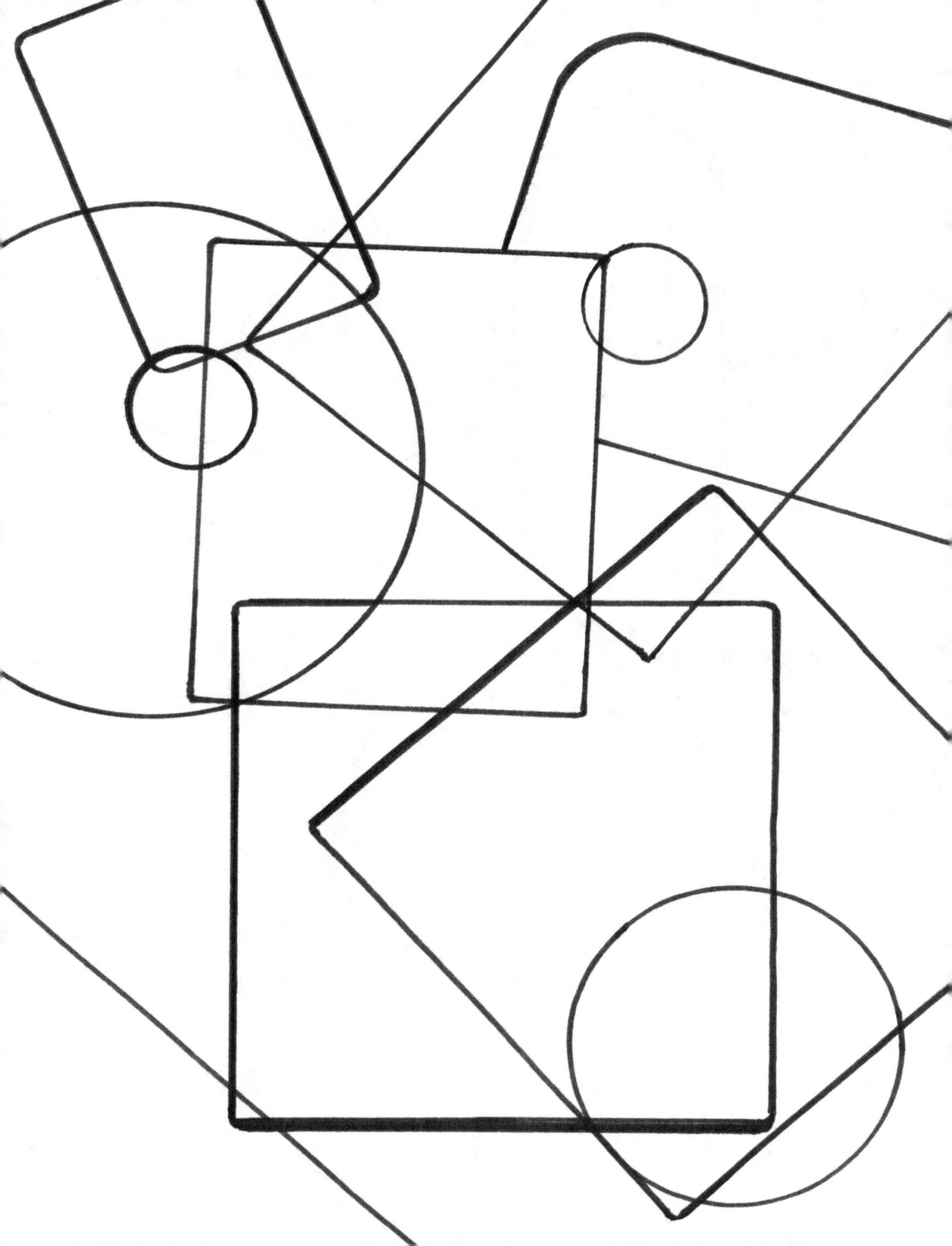

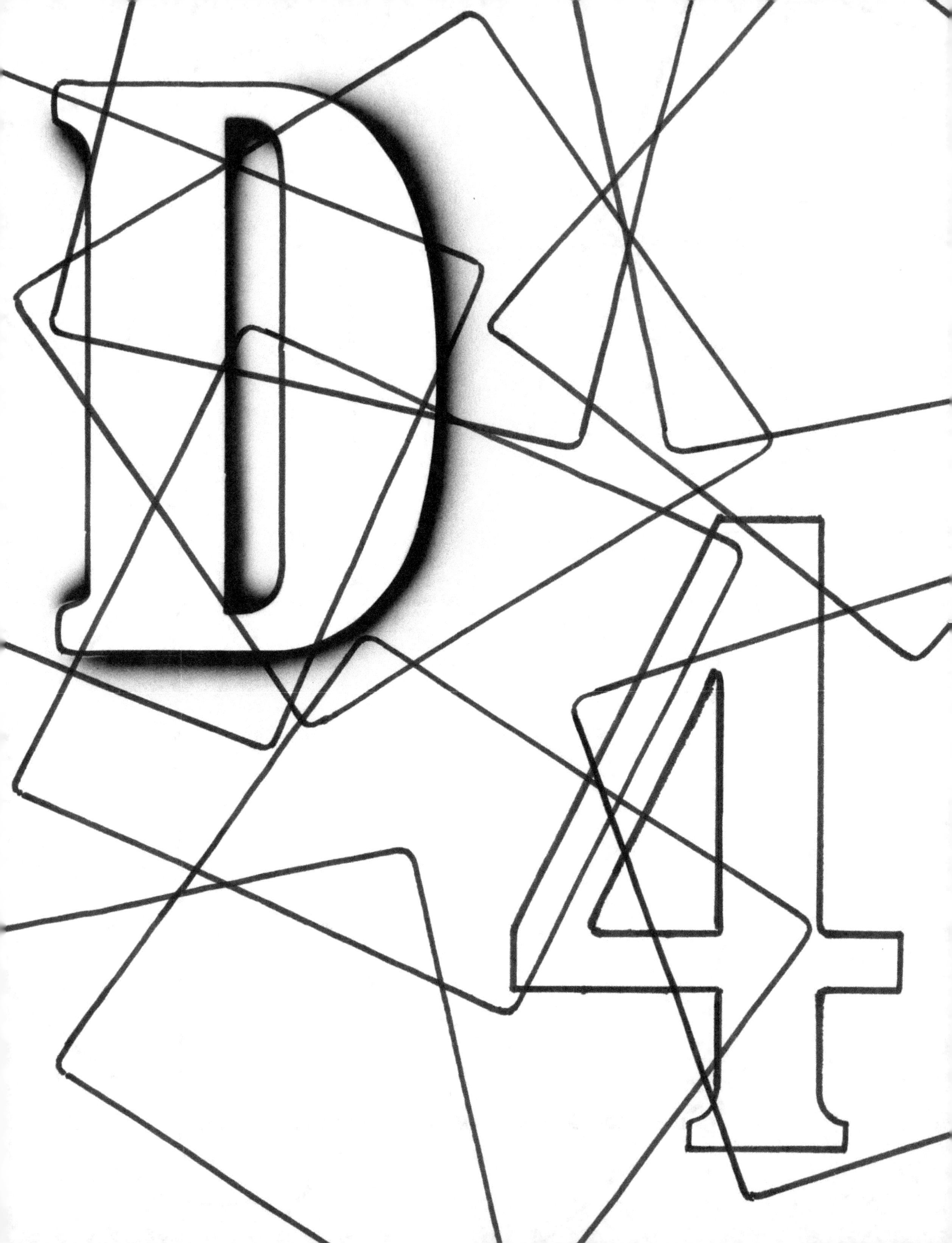

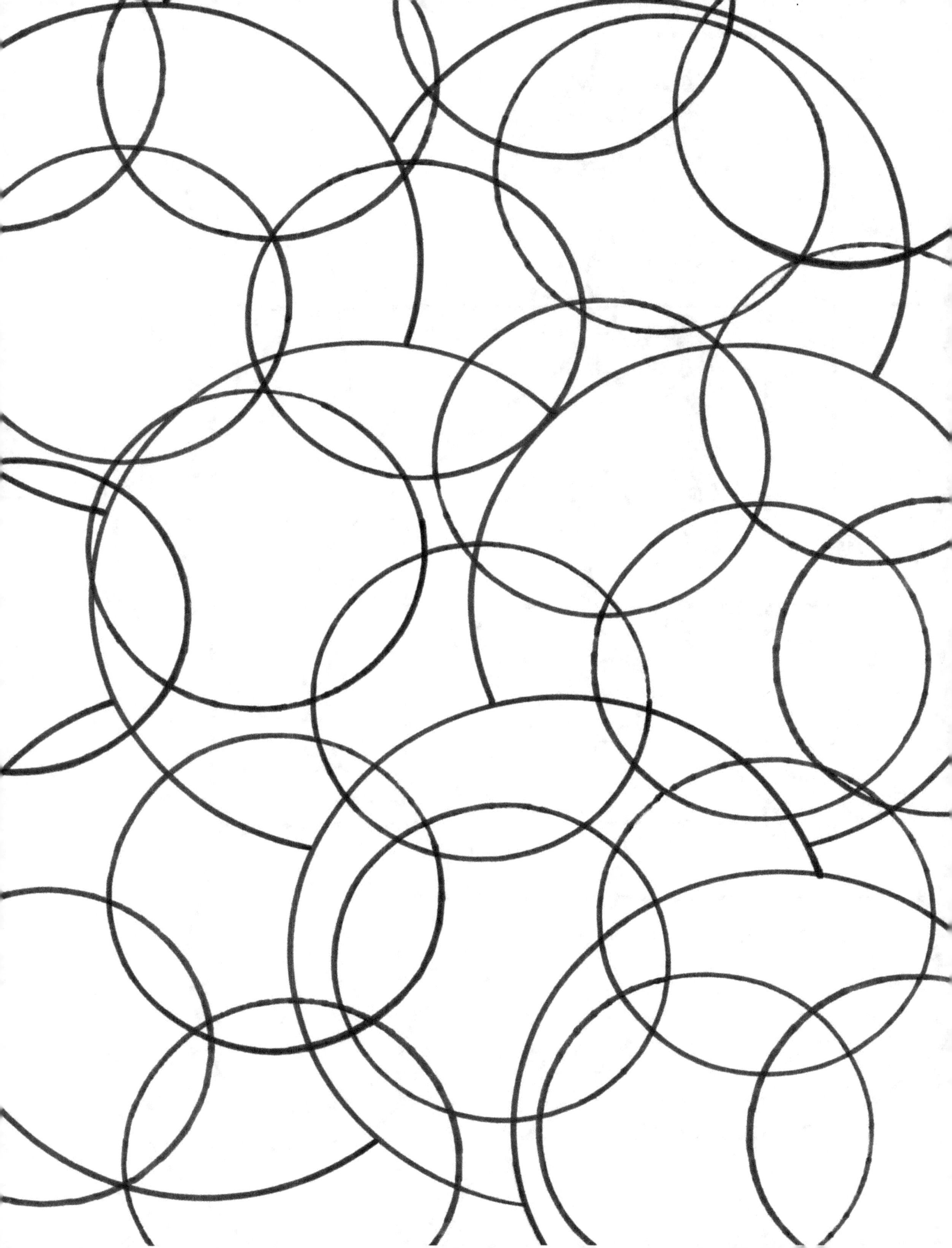

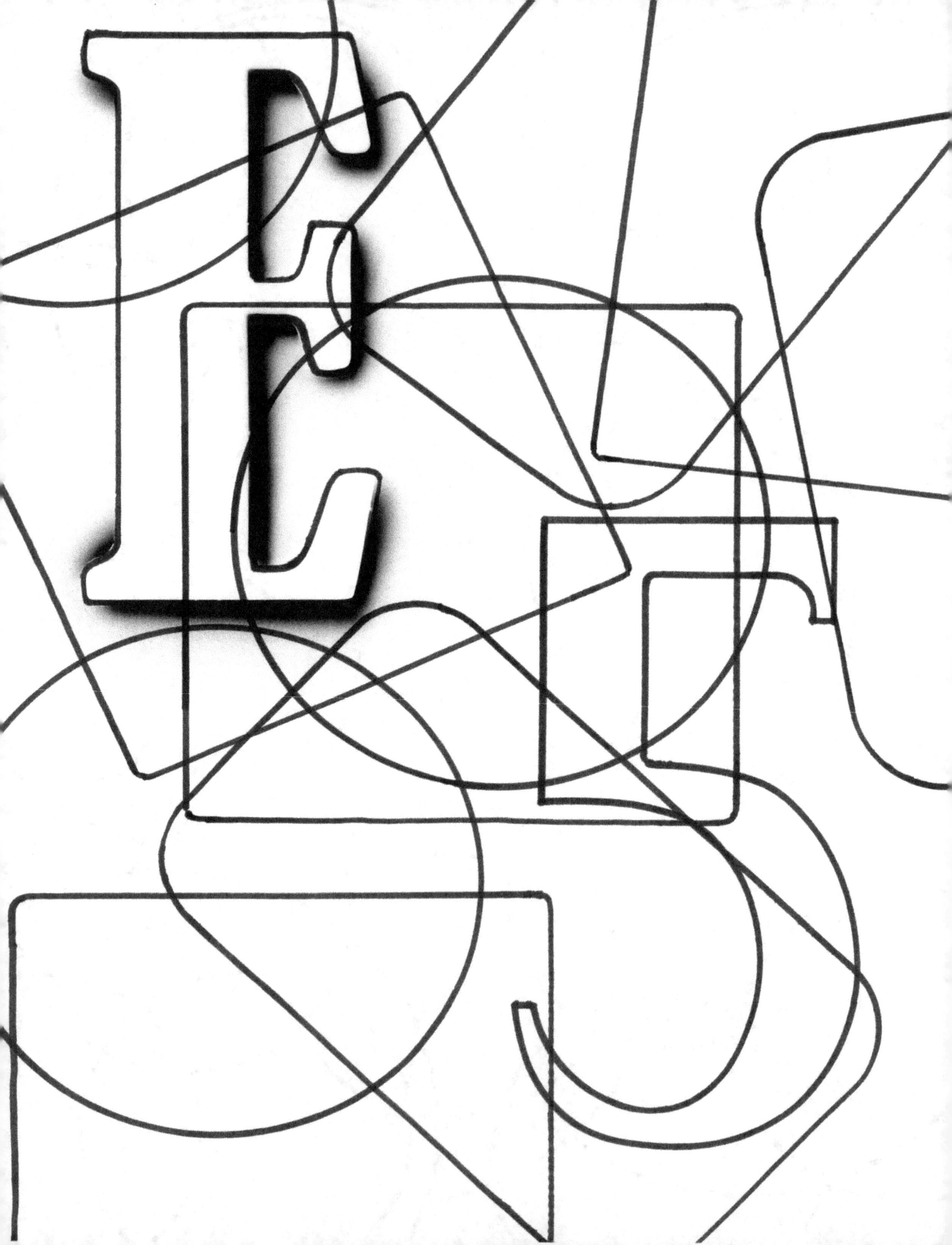

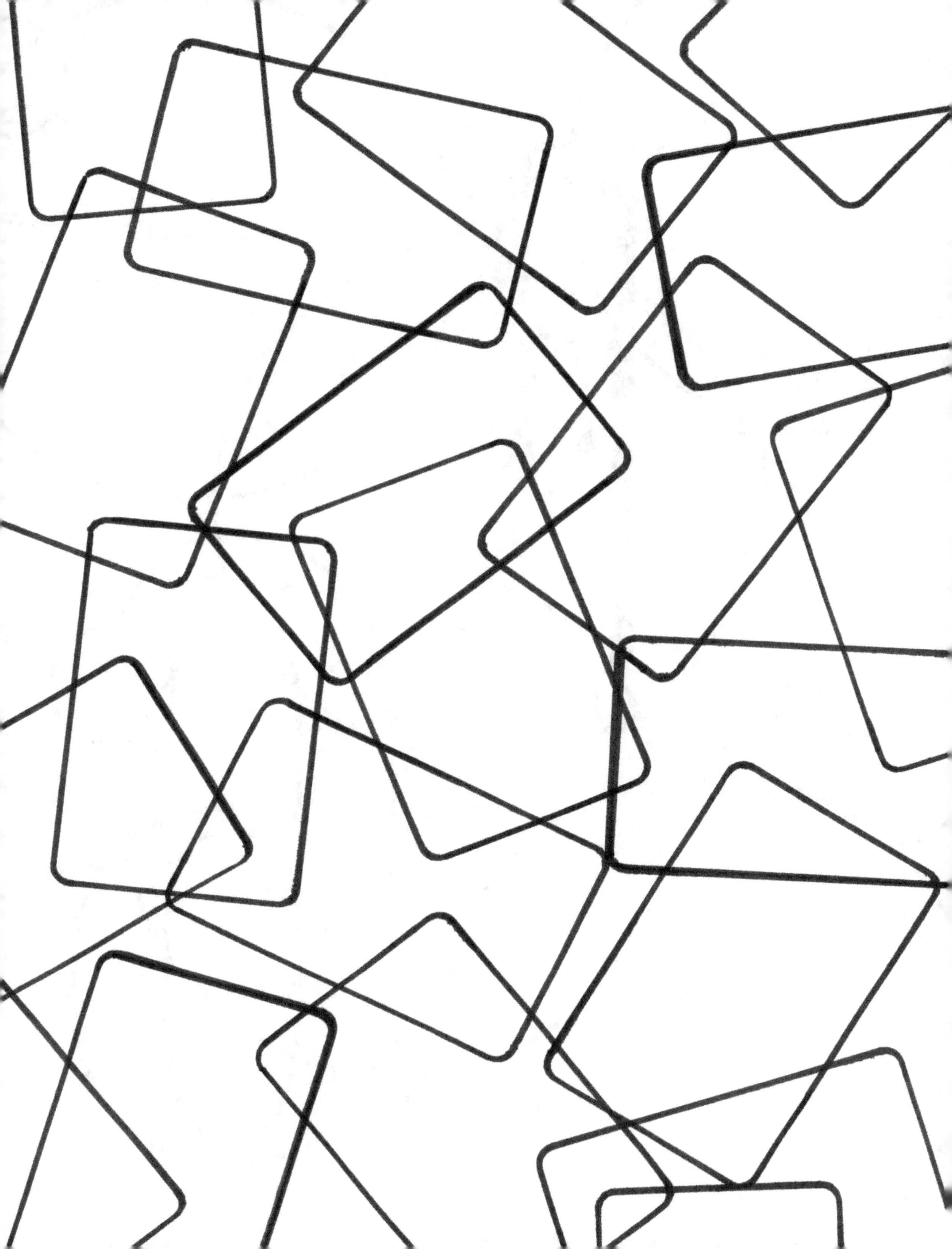

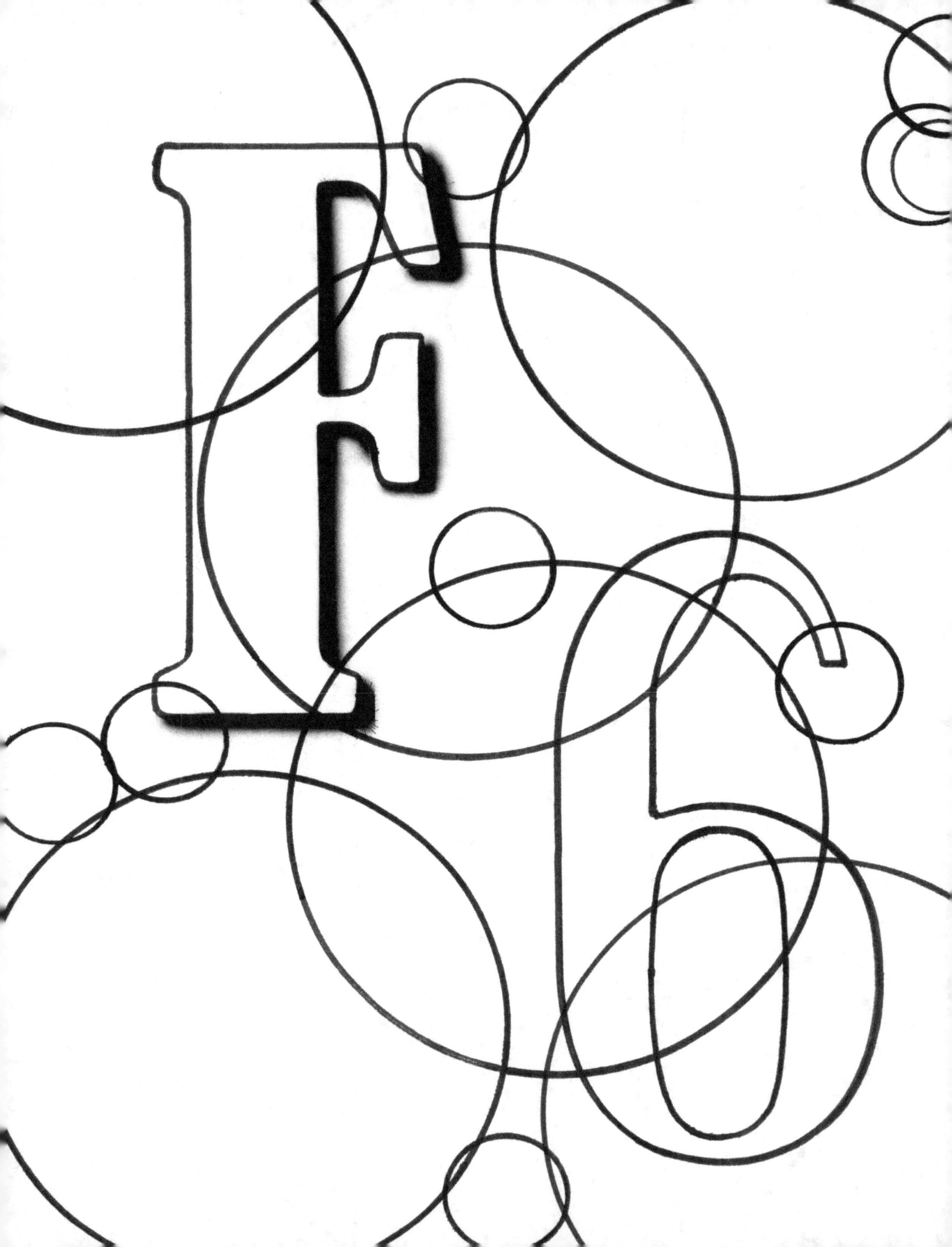

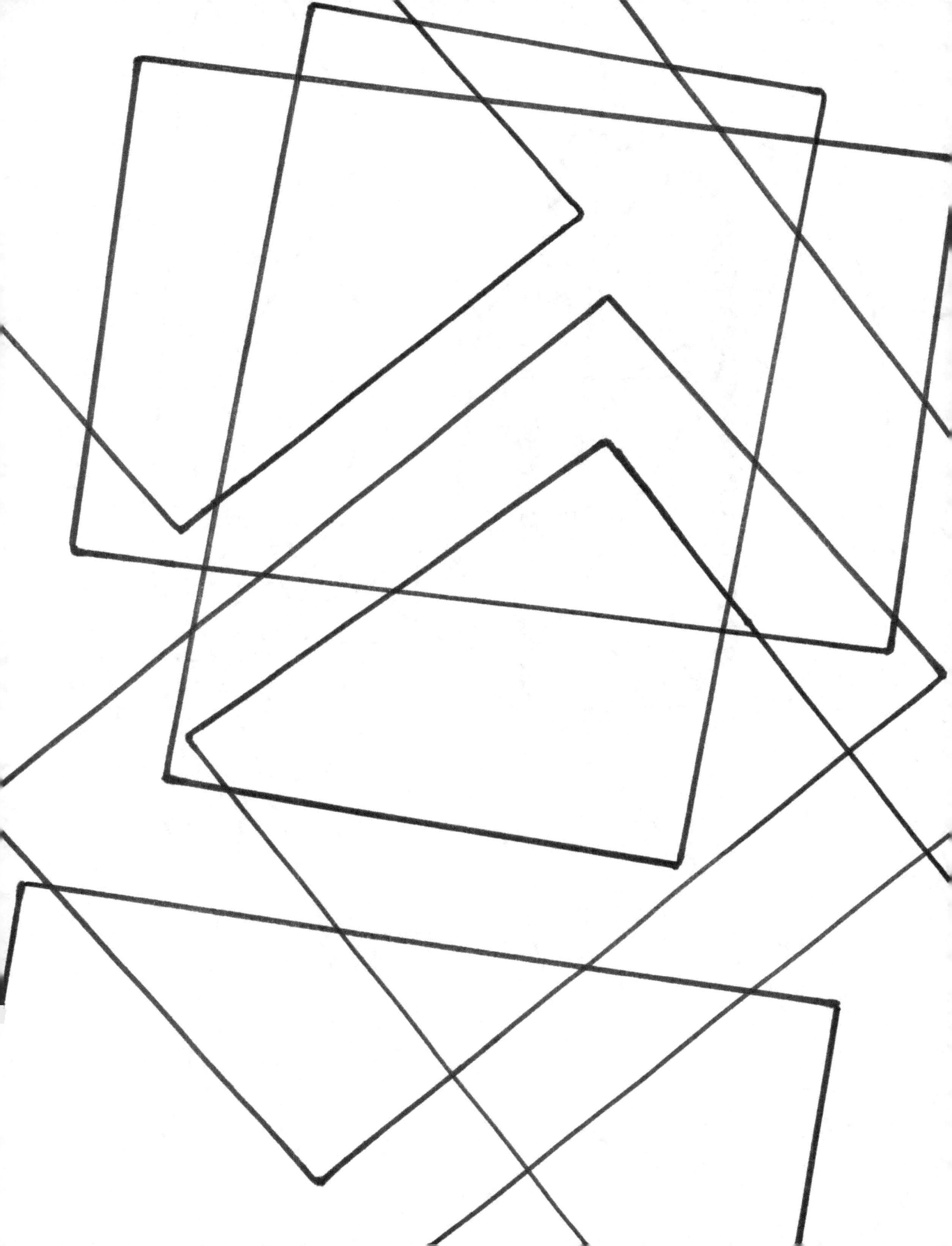

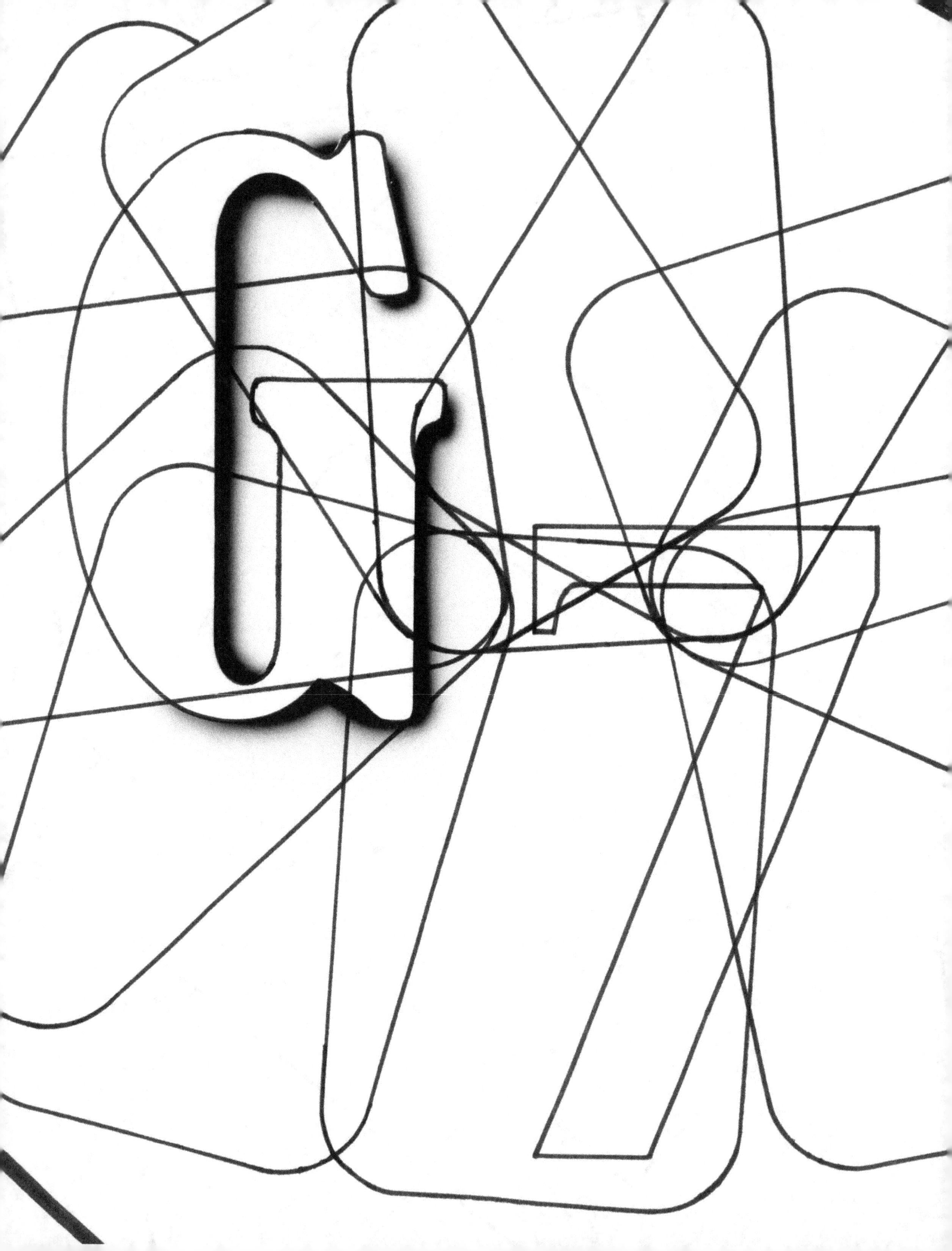

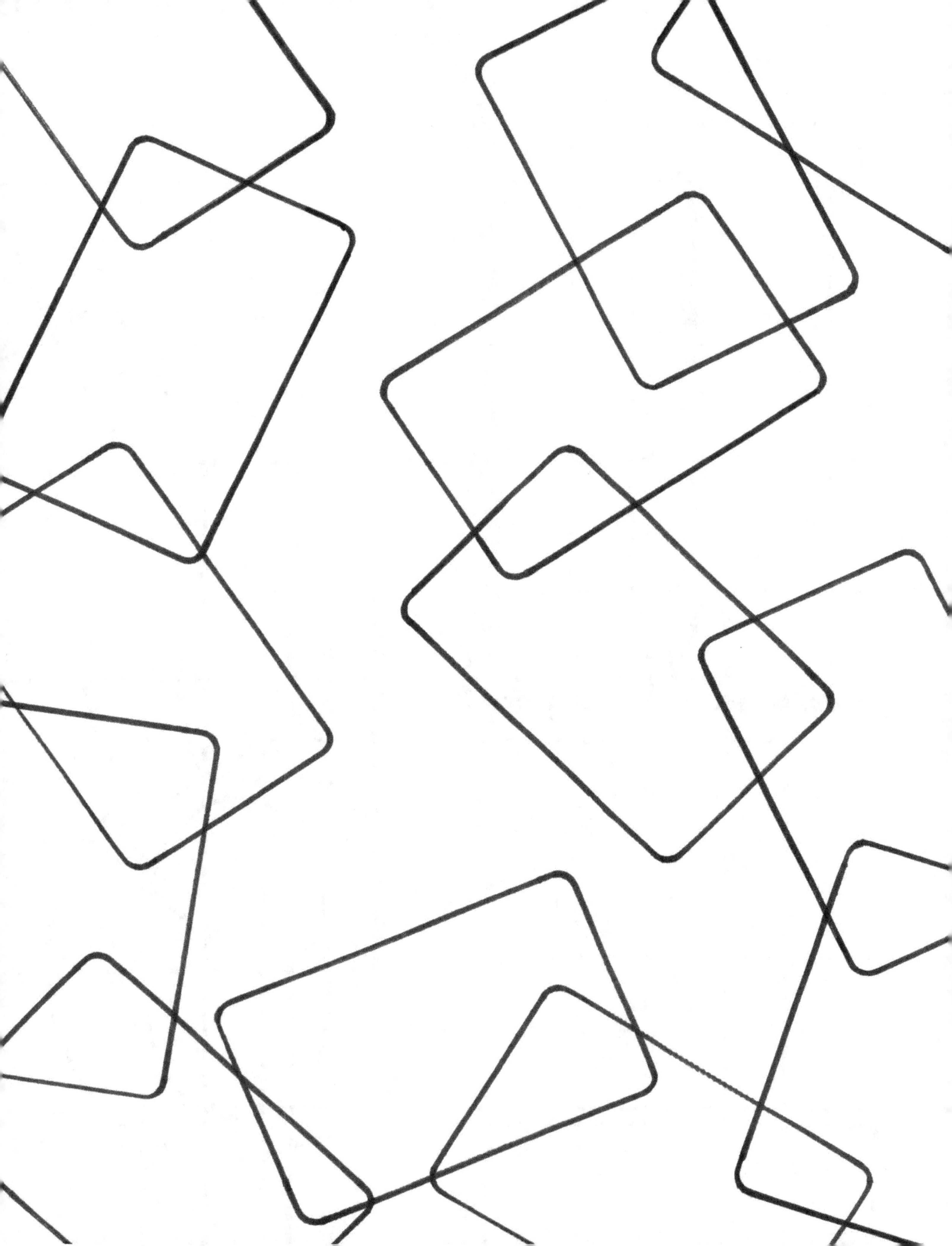

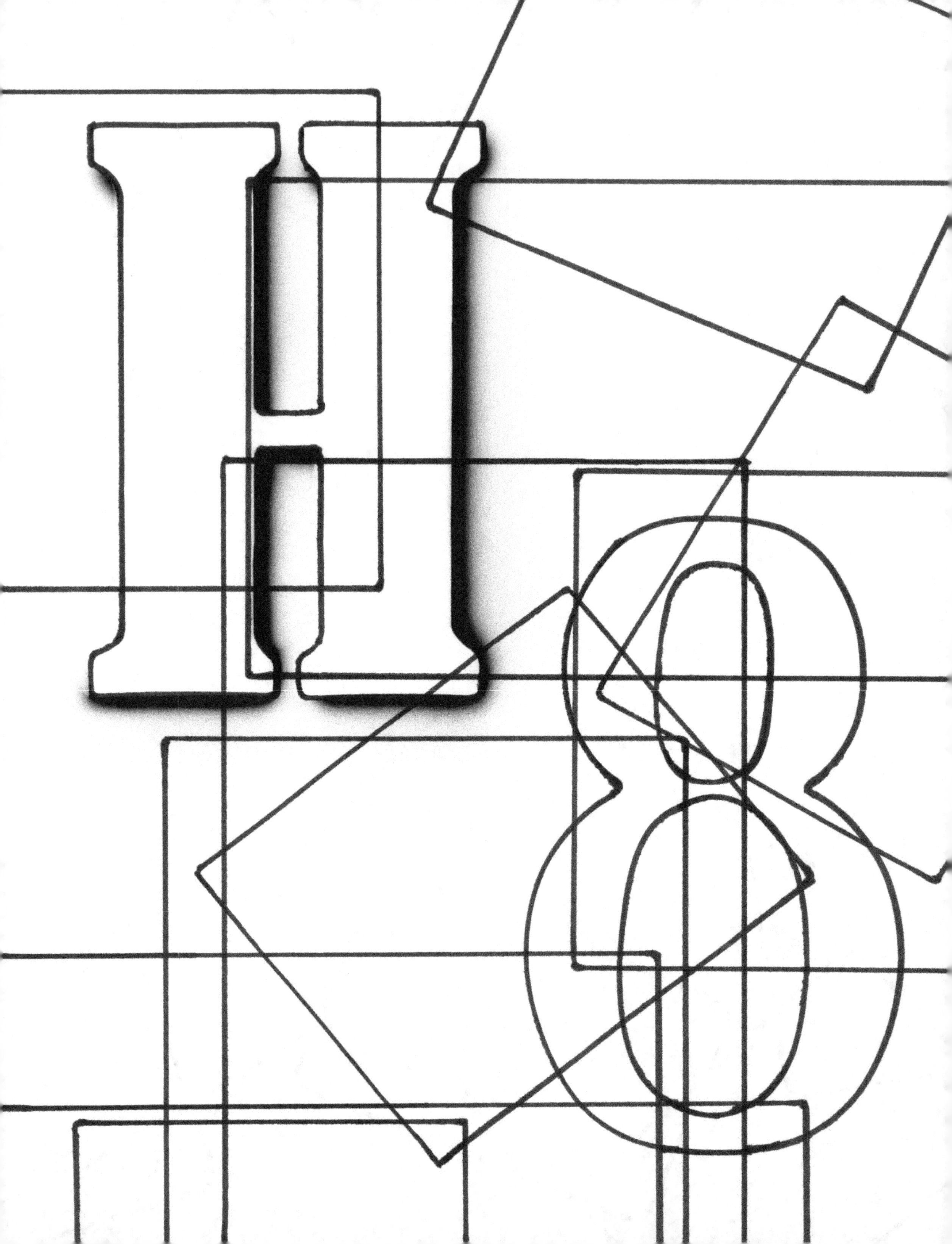

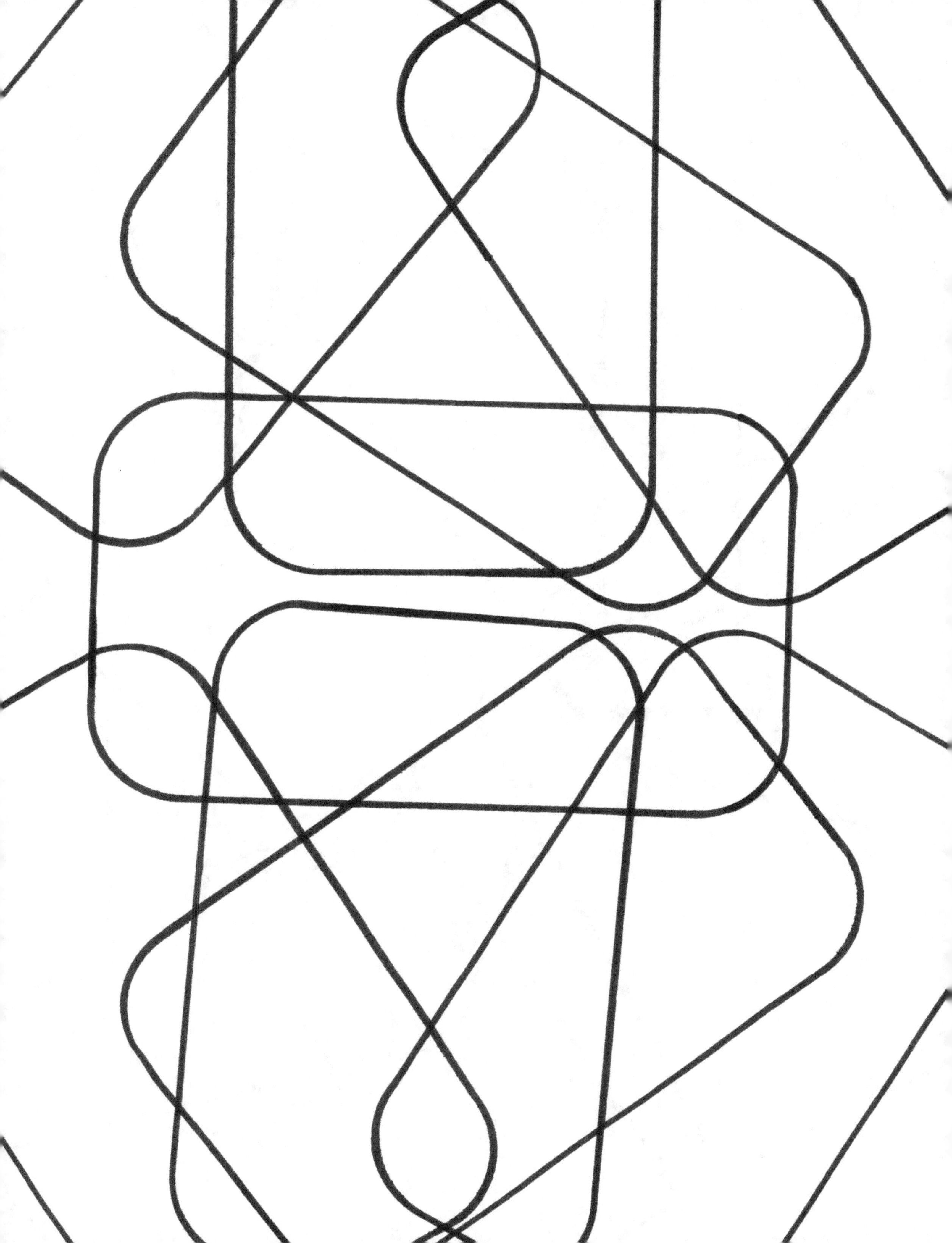

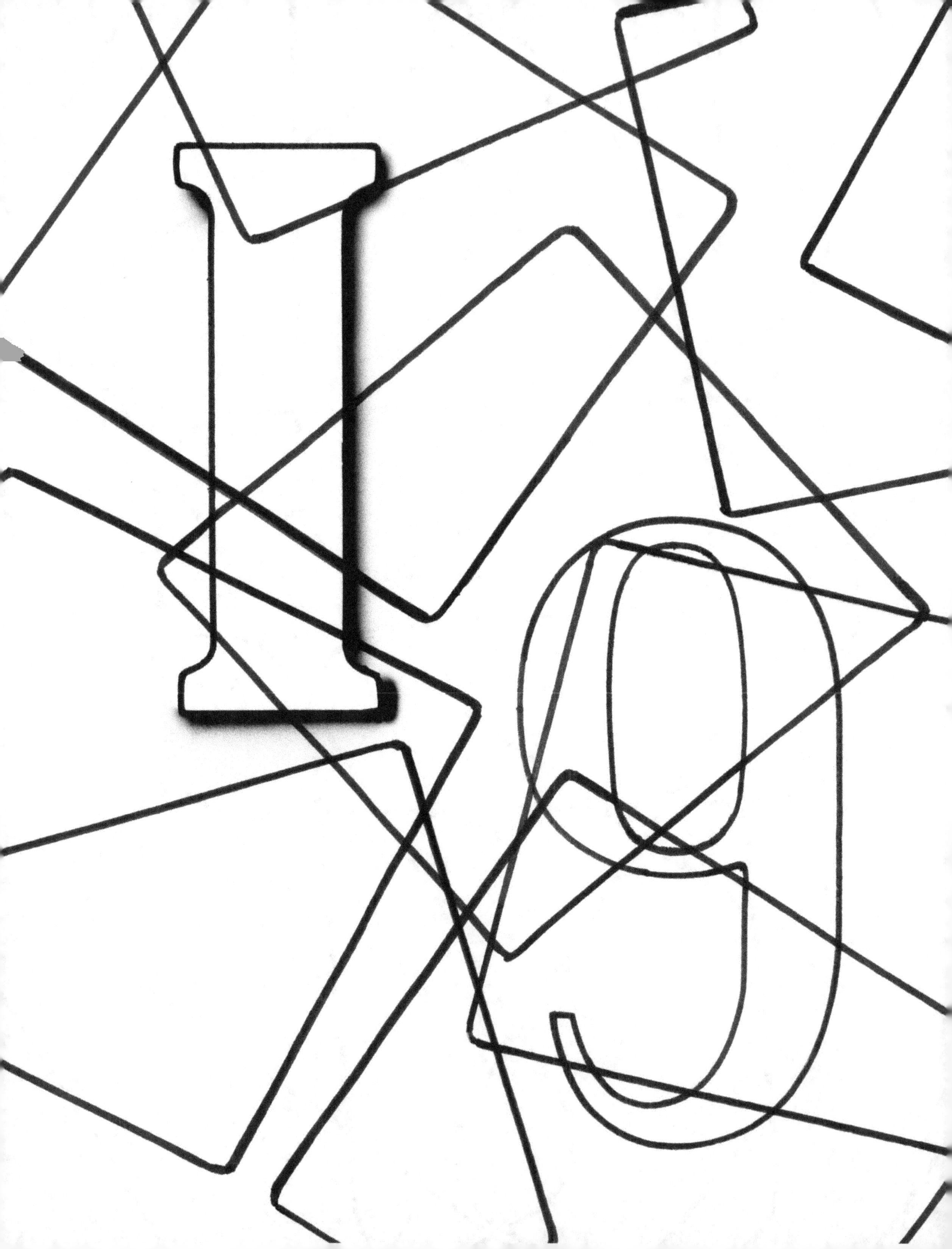

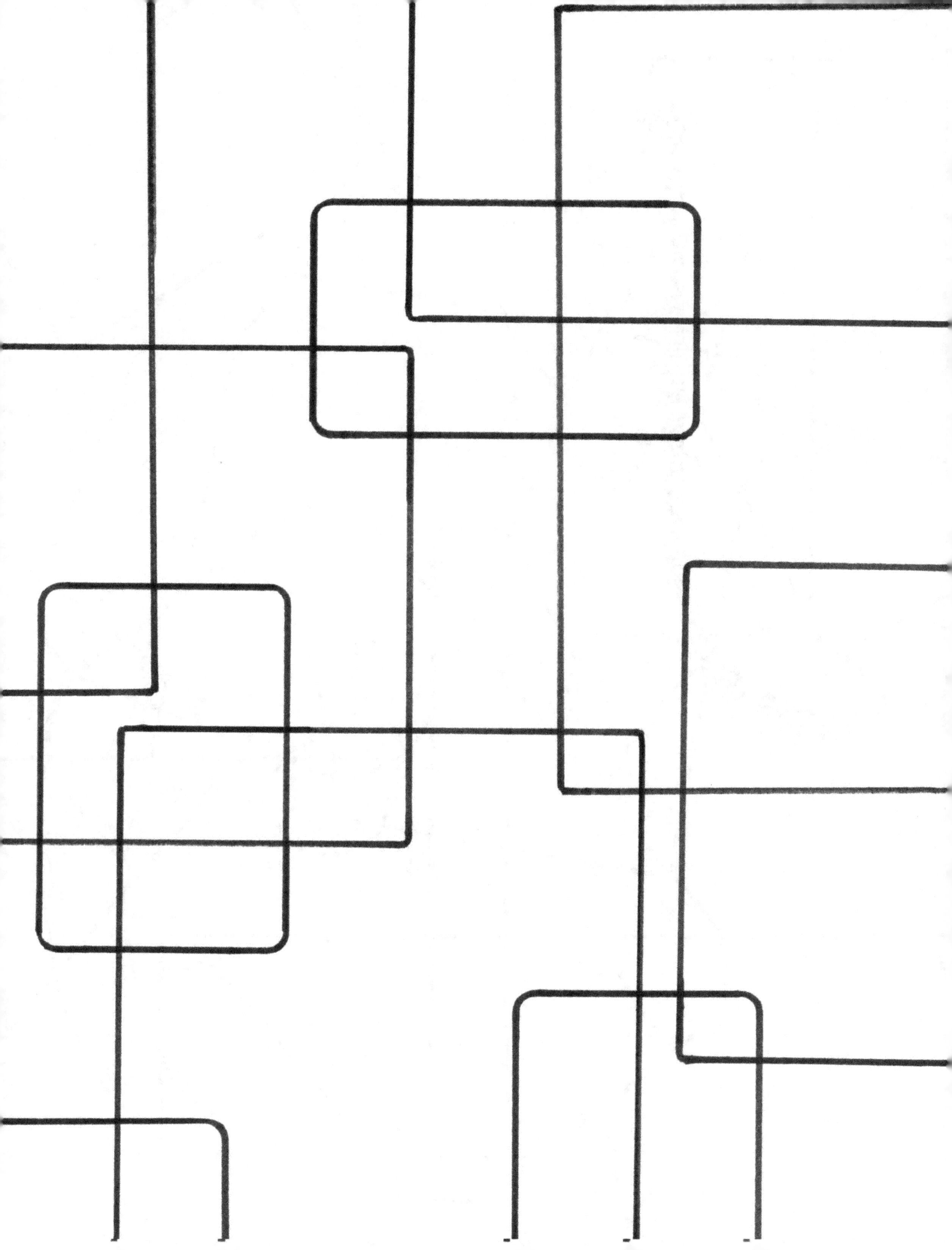

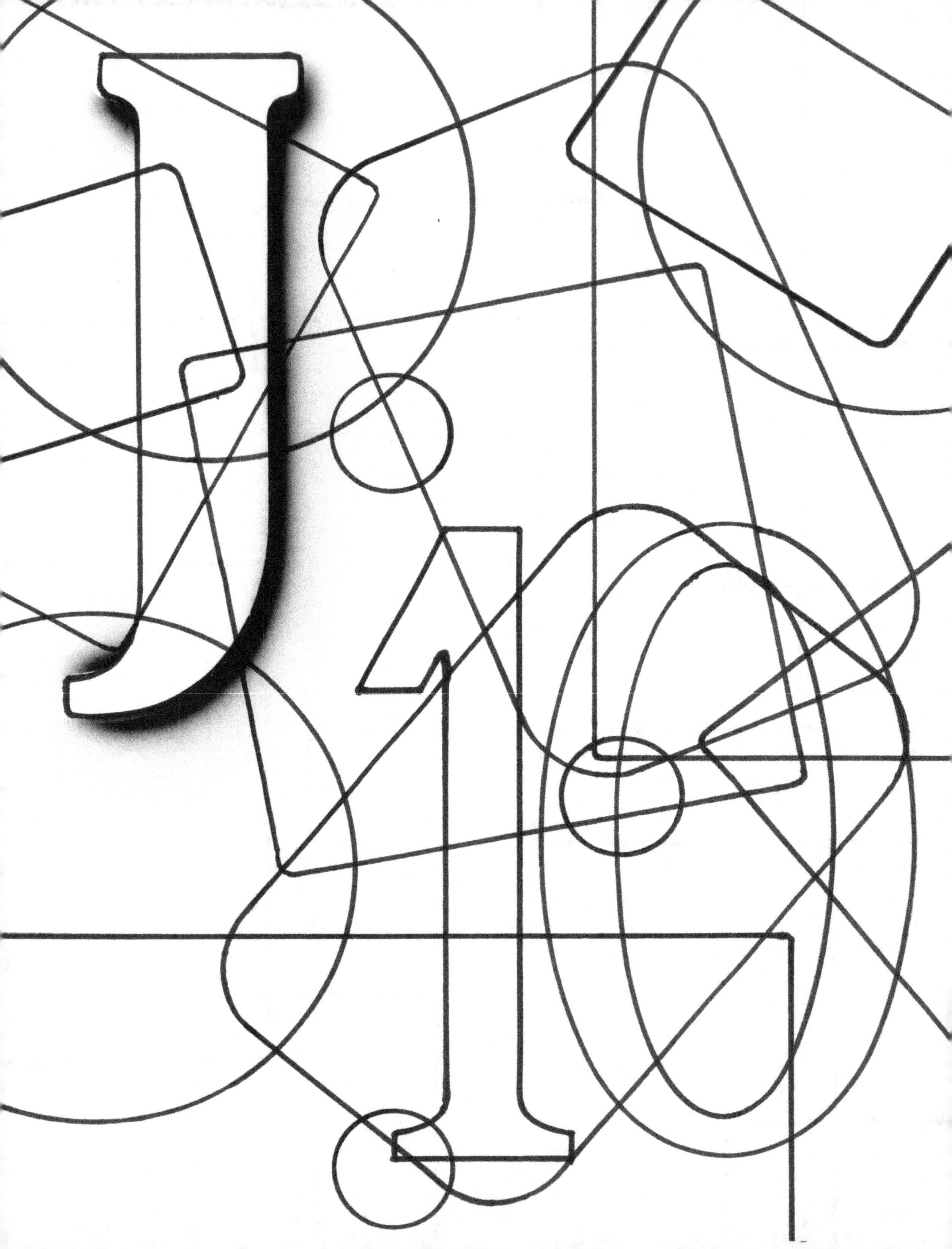

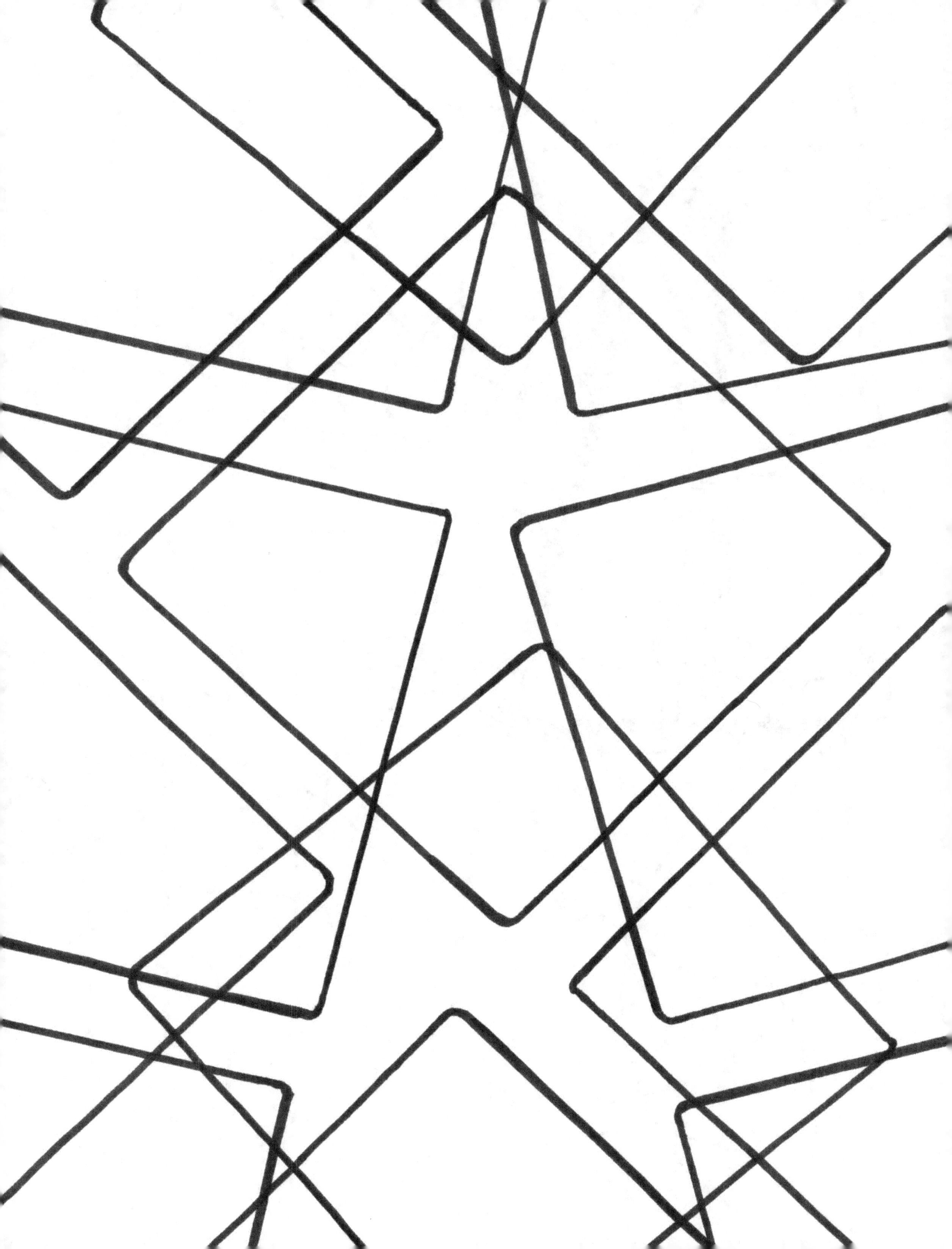

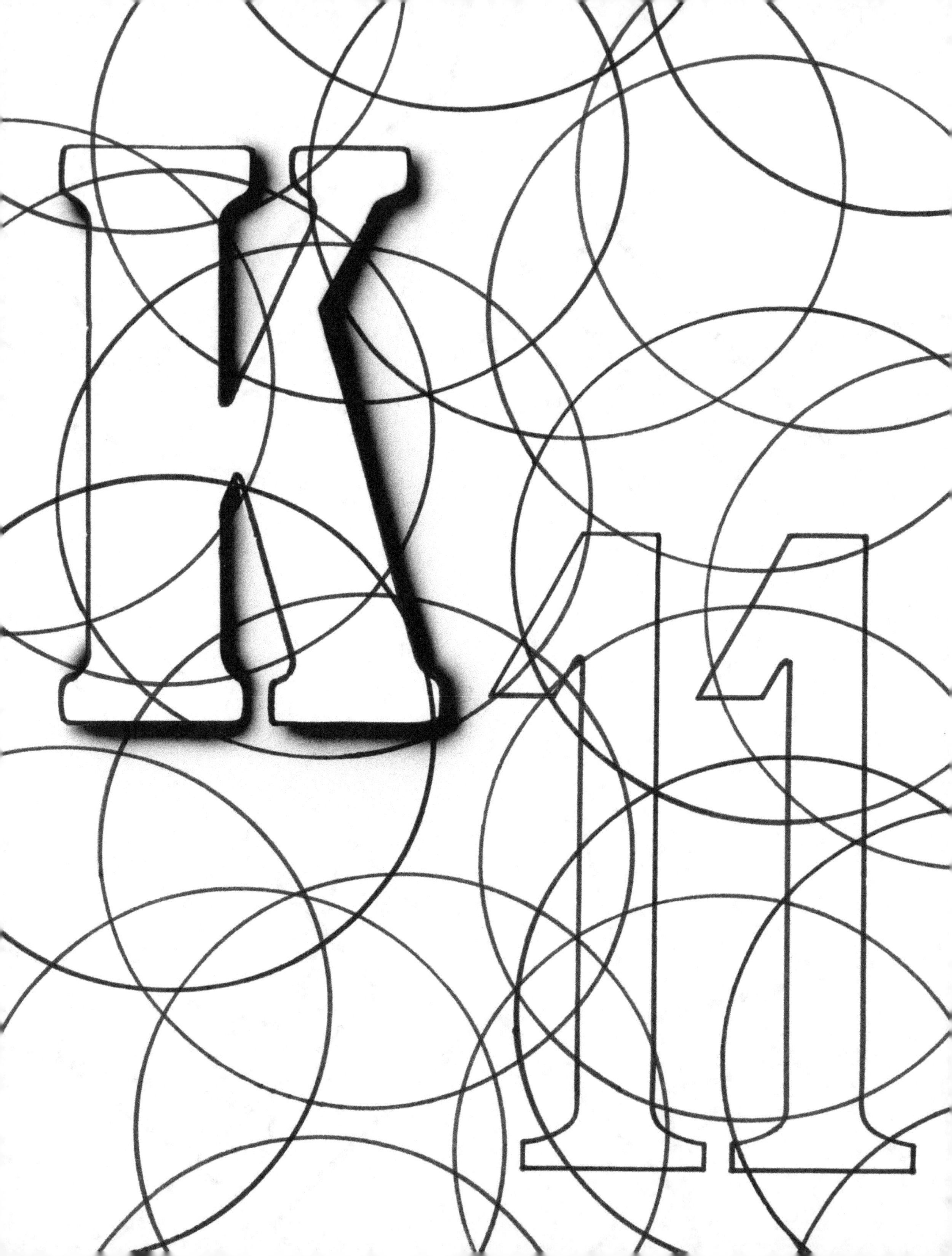

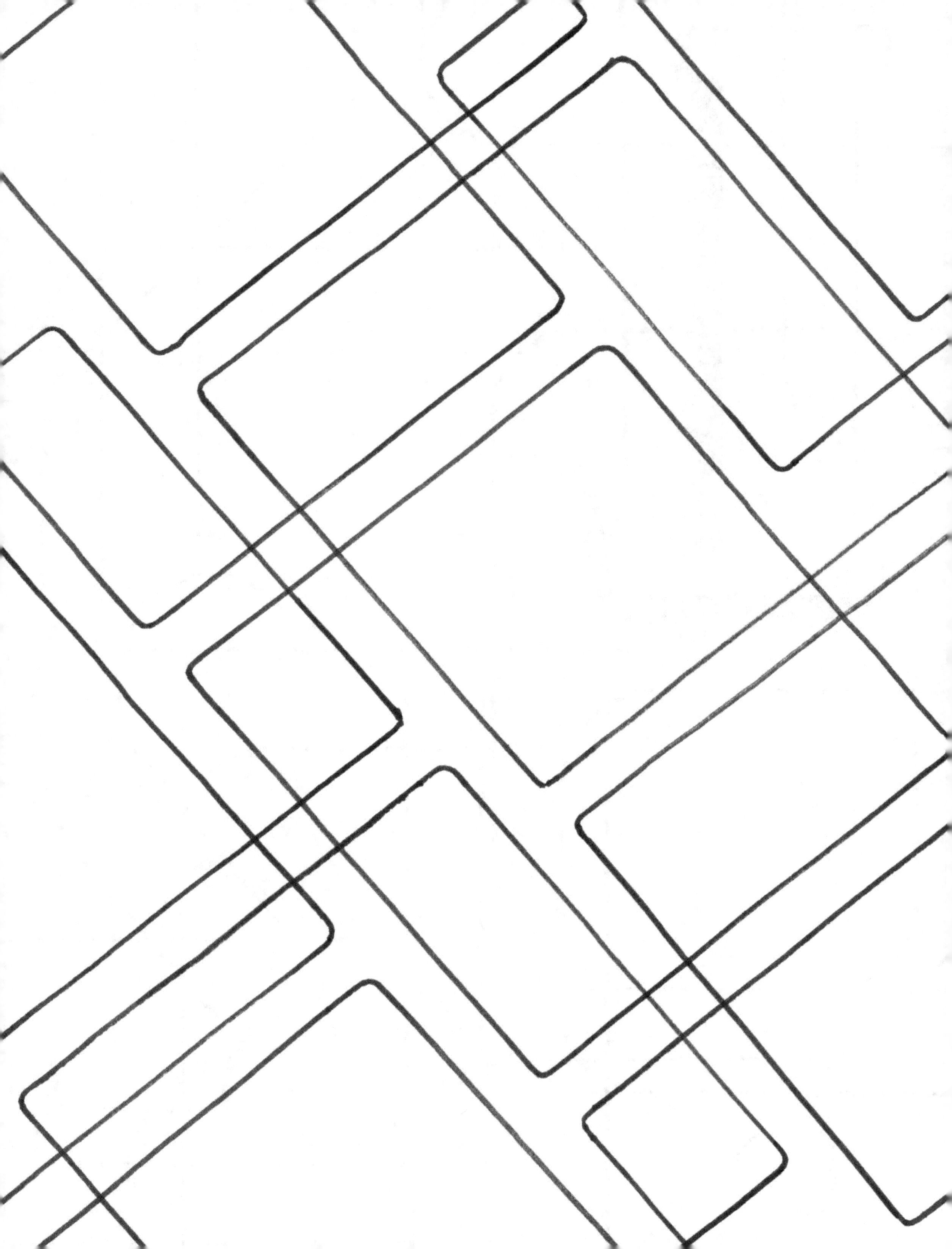

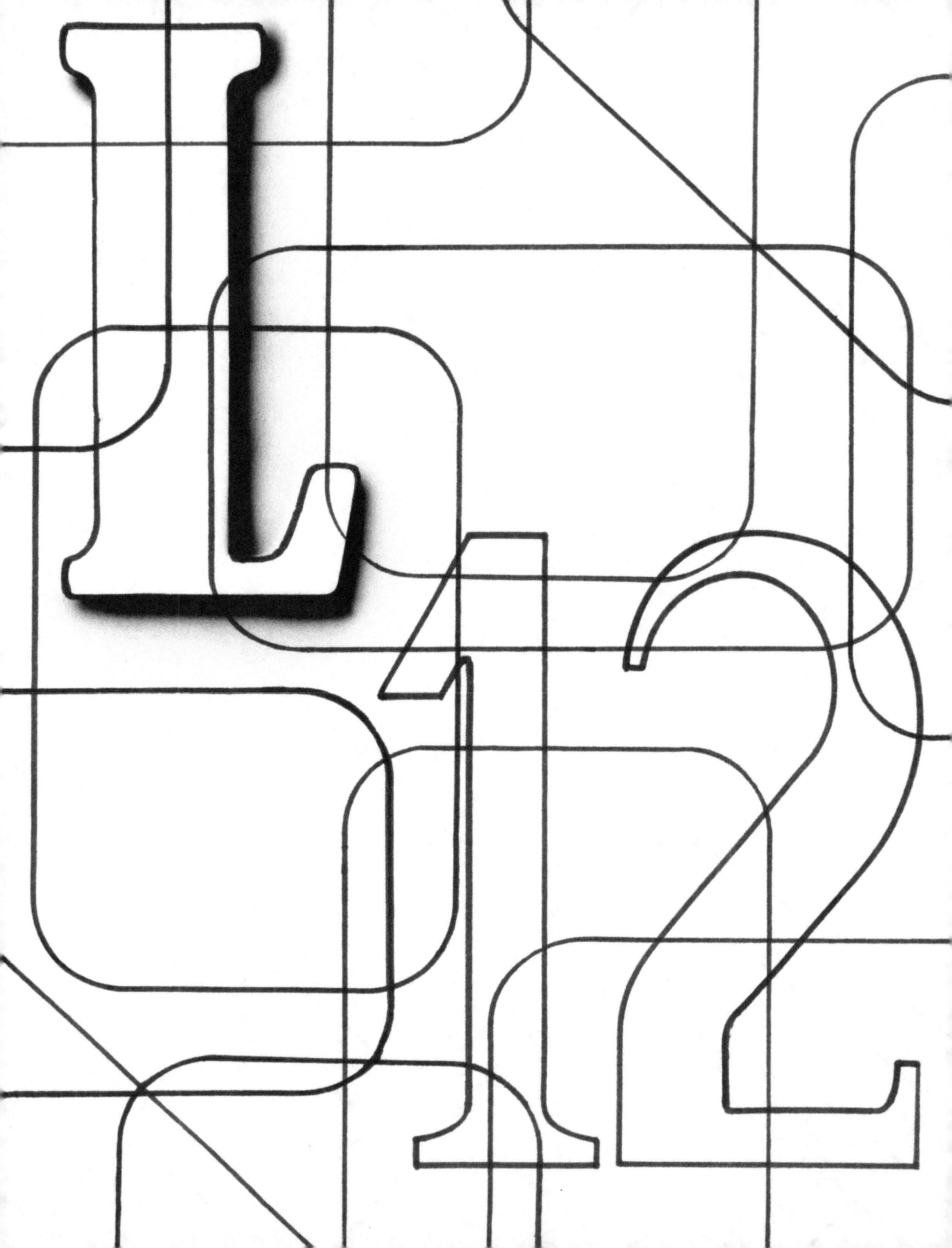

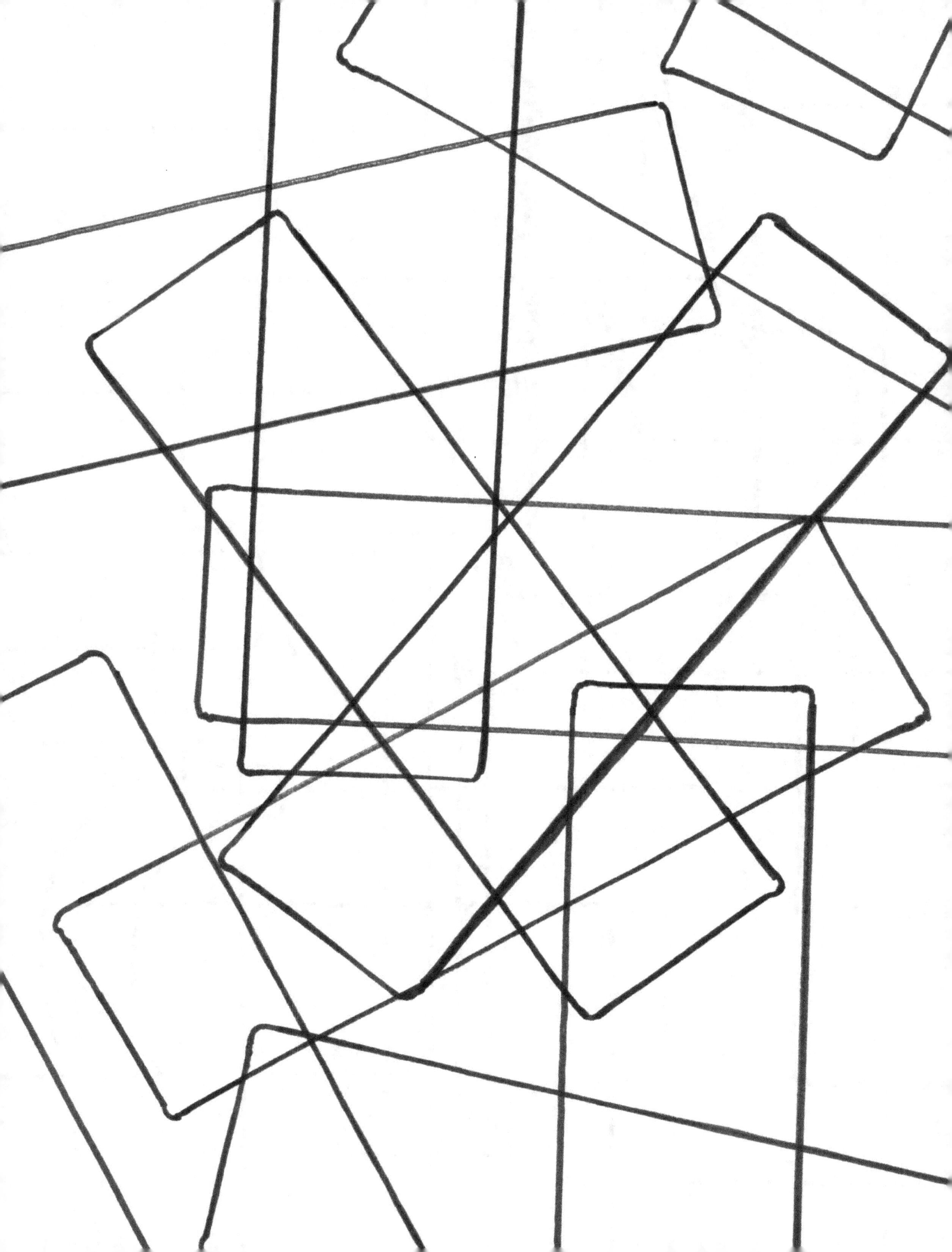

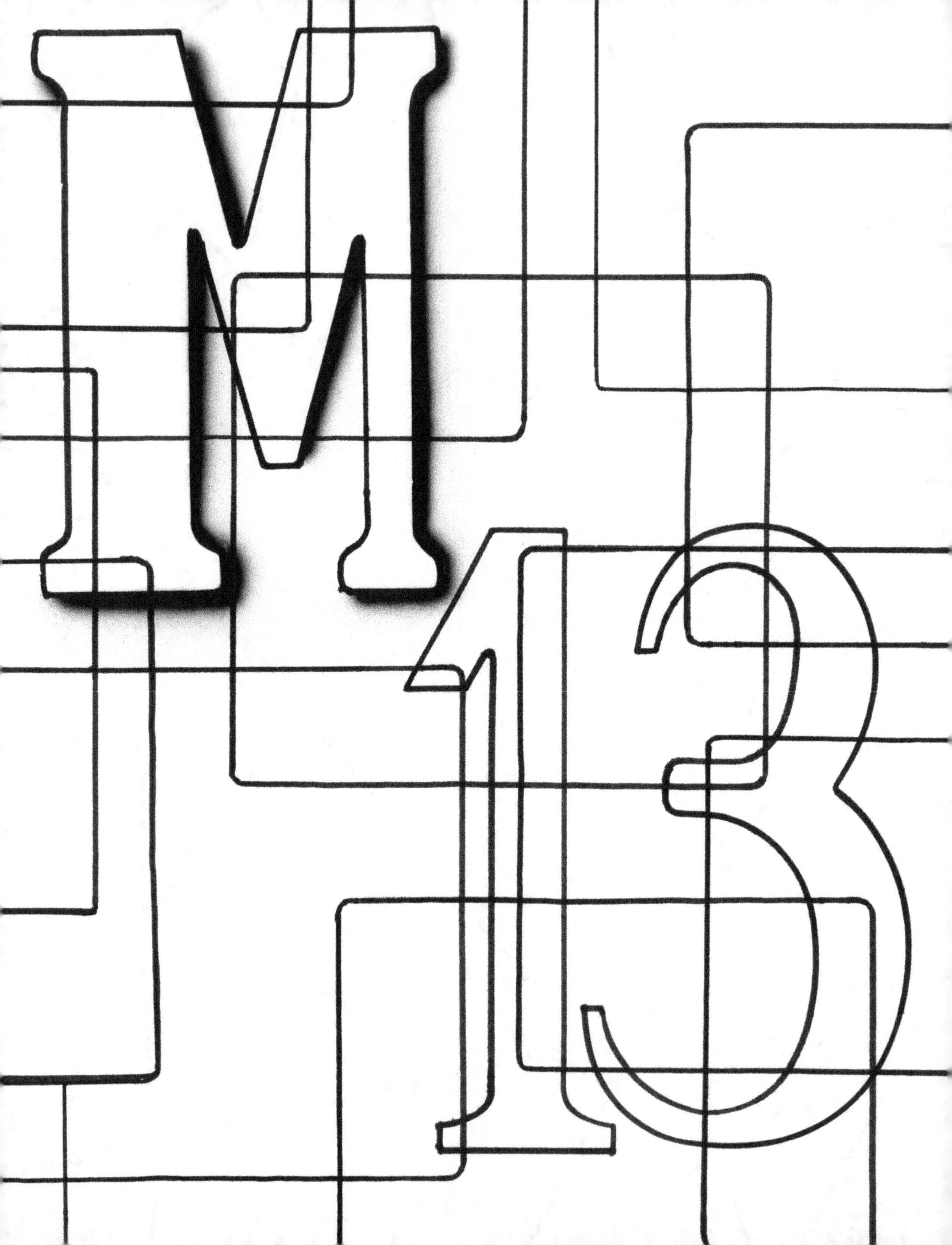
M
13

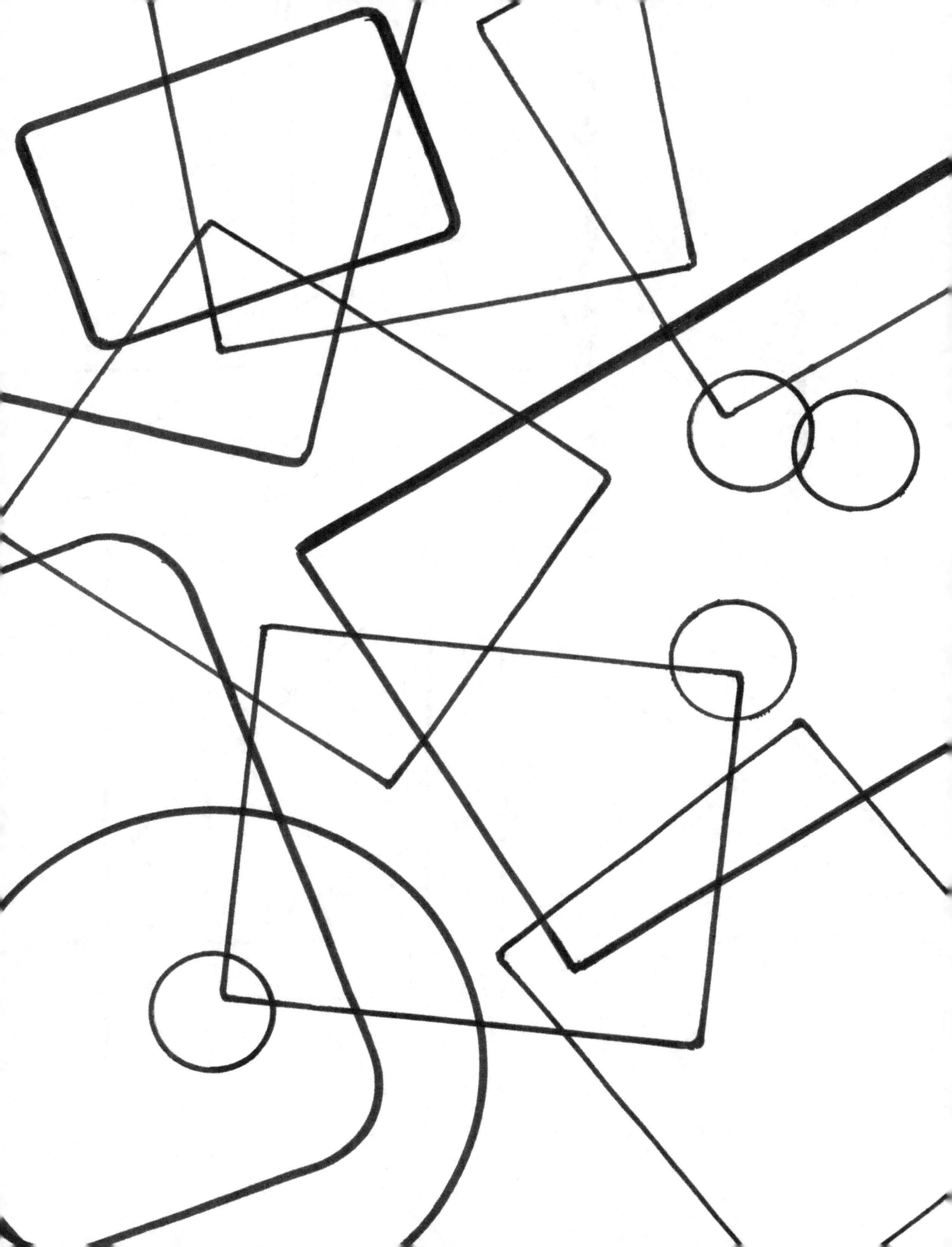

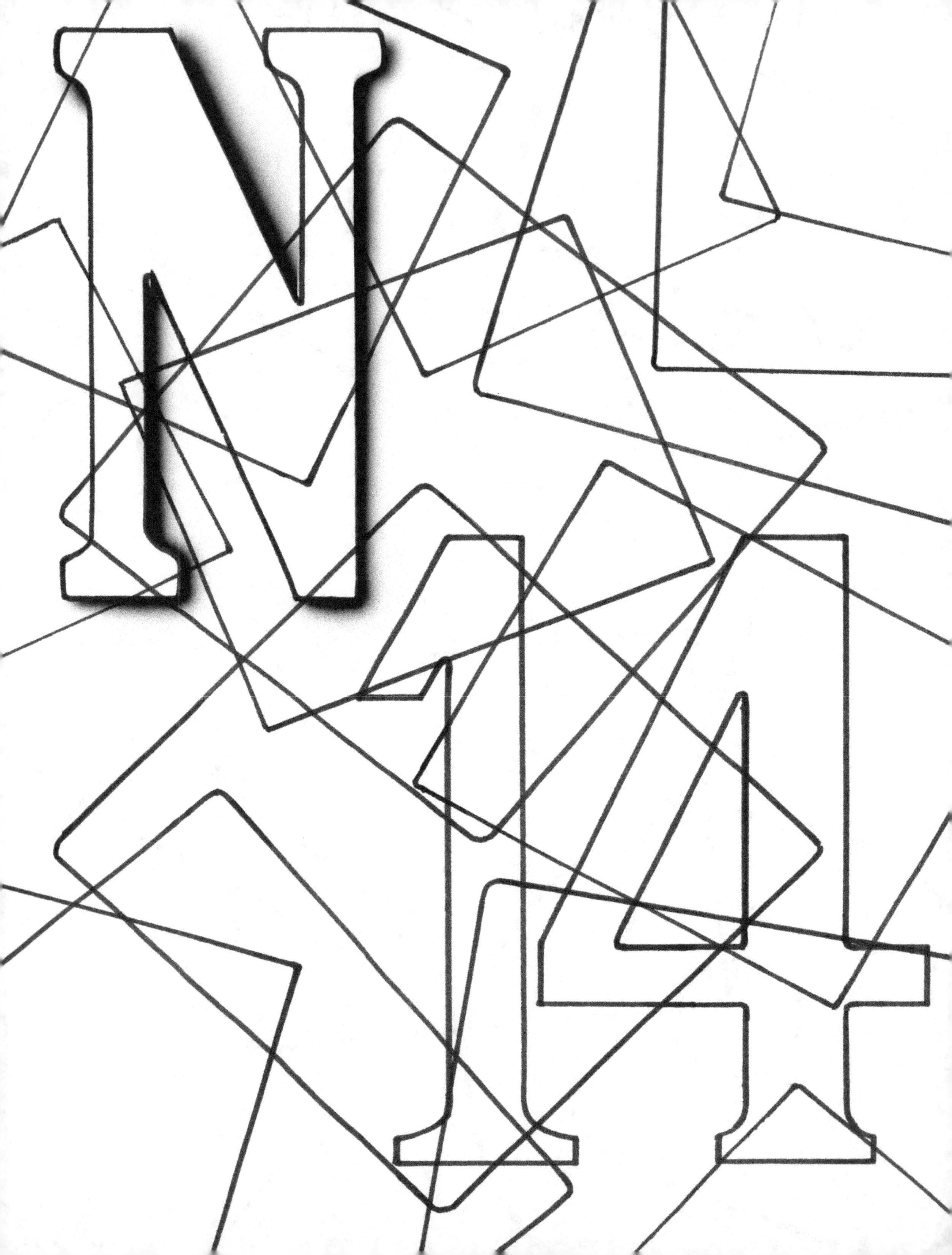

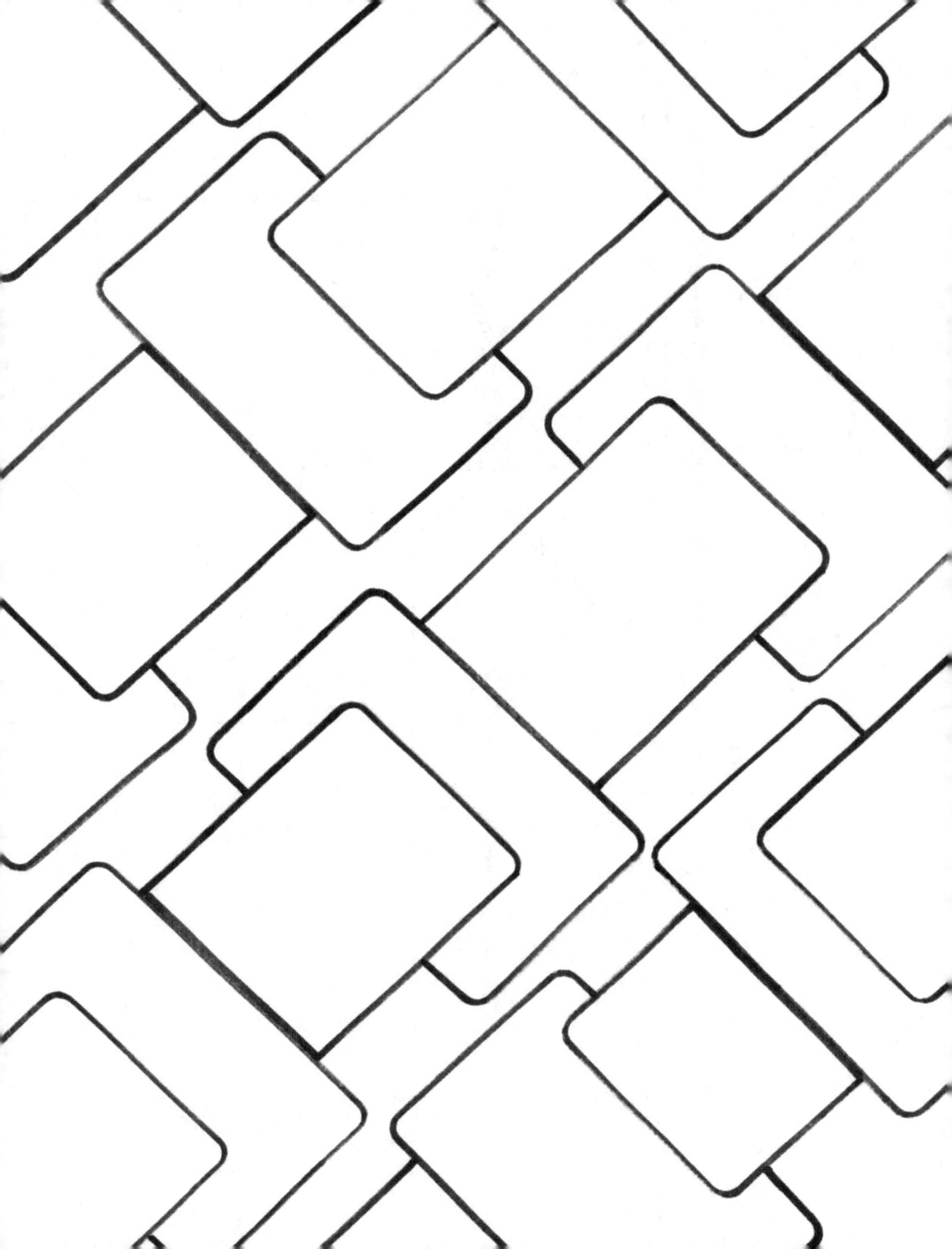

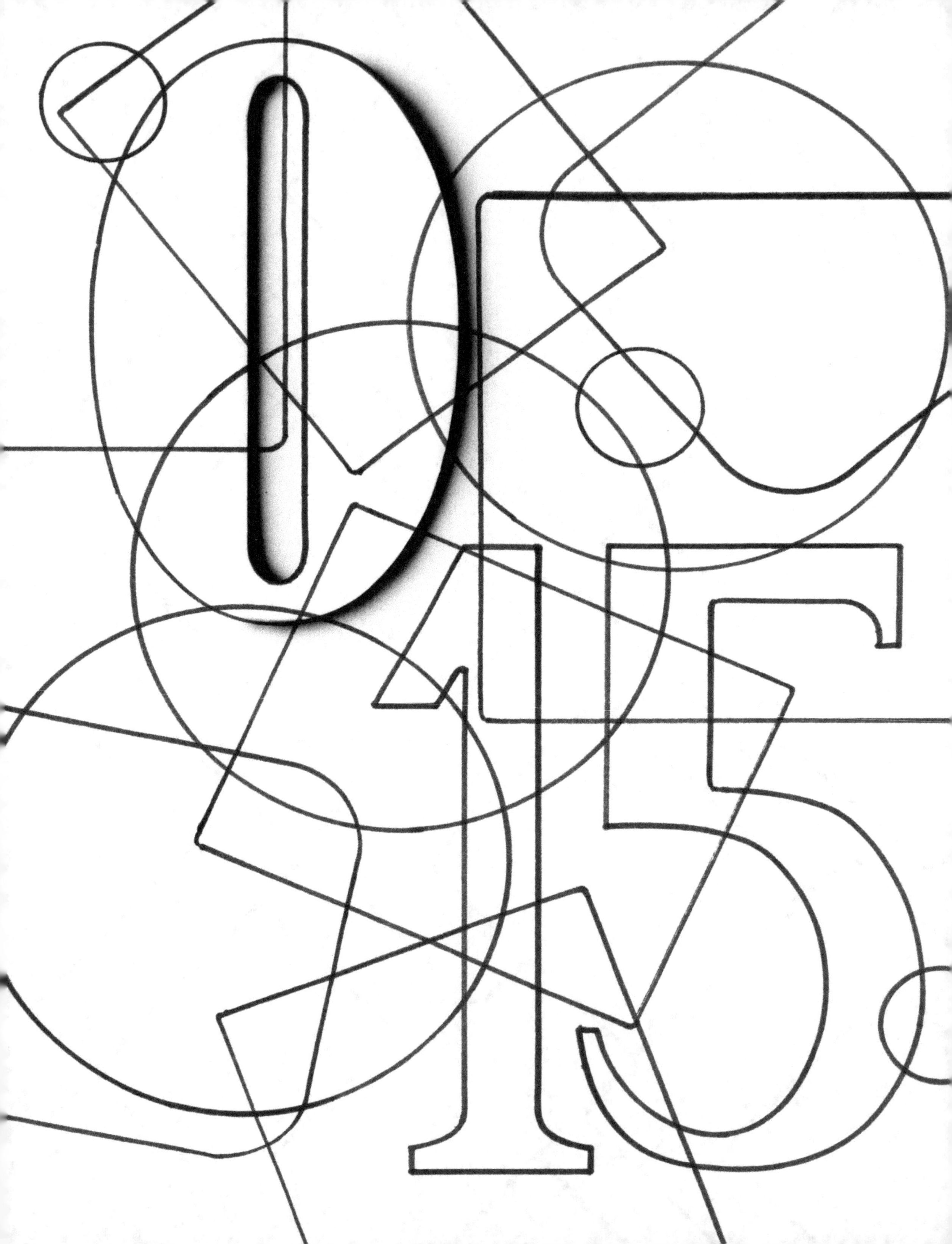

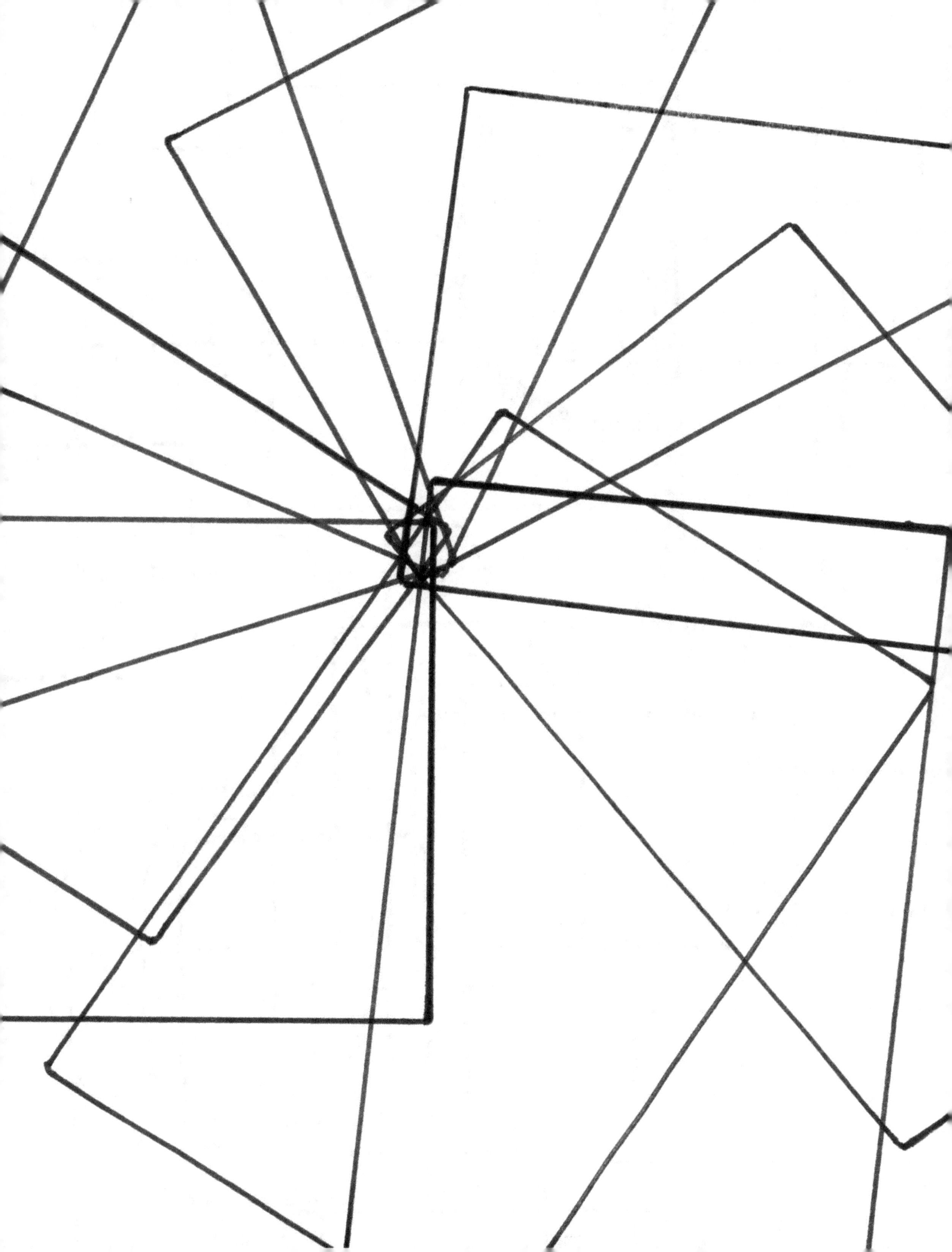

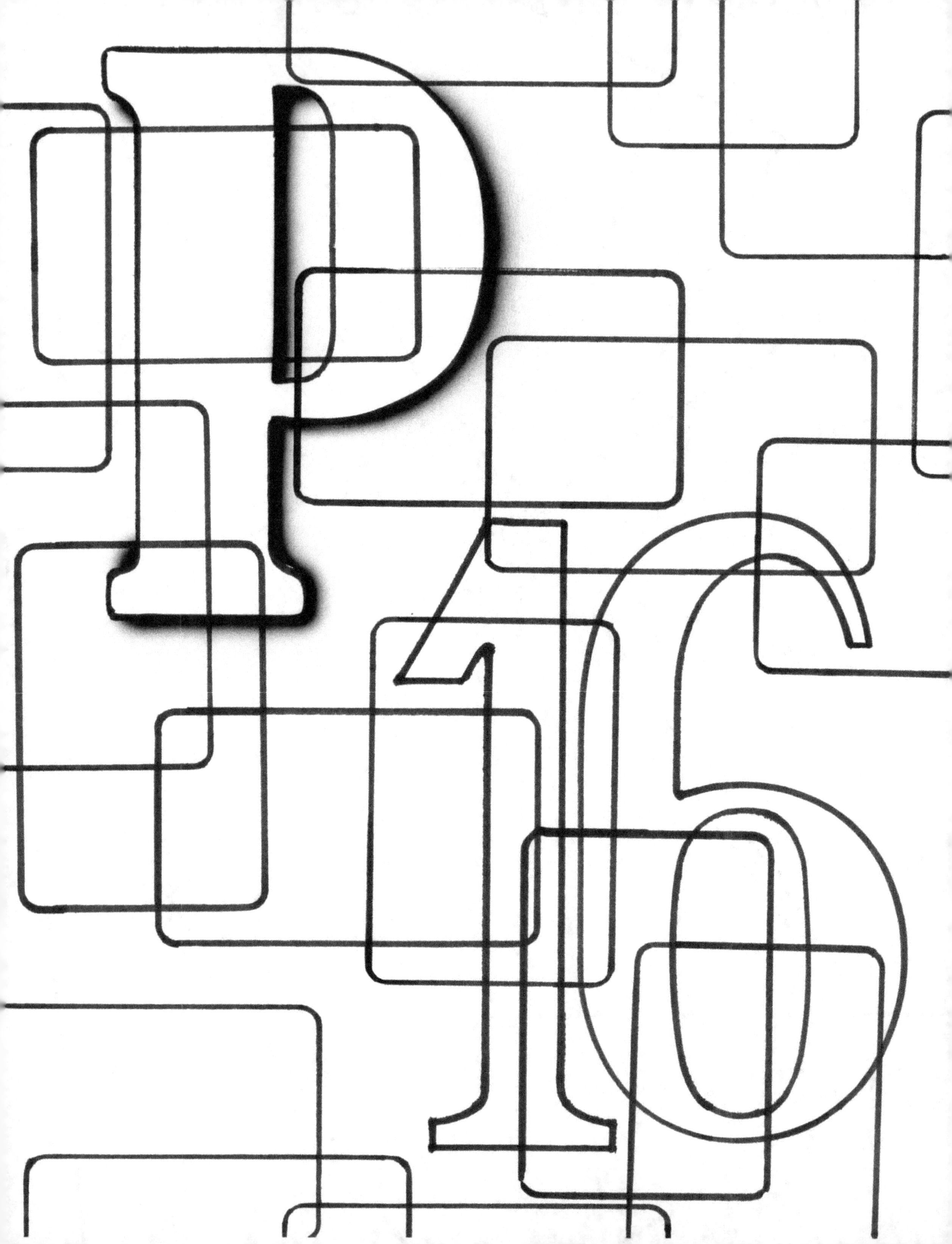

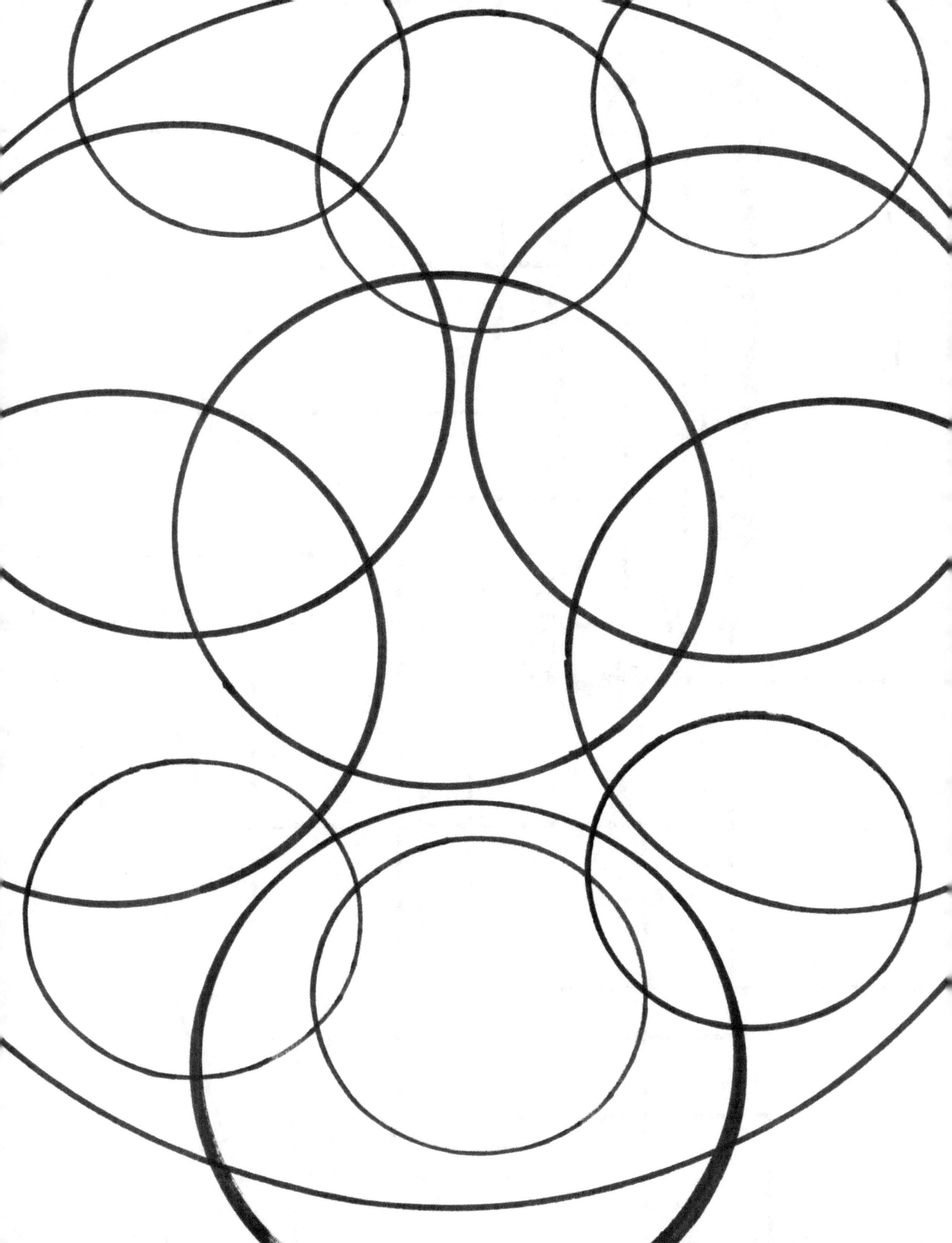

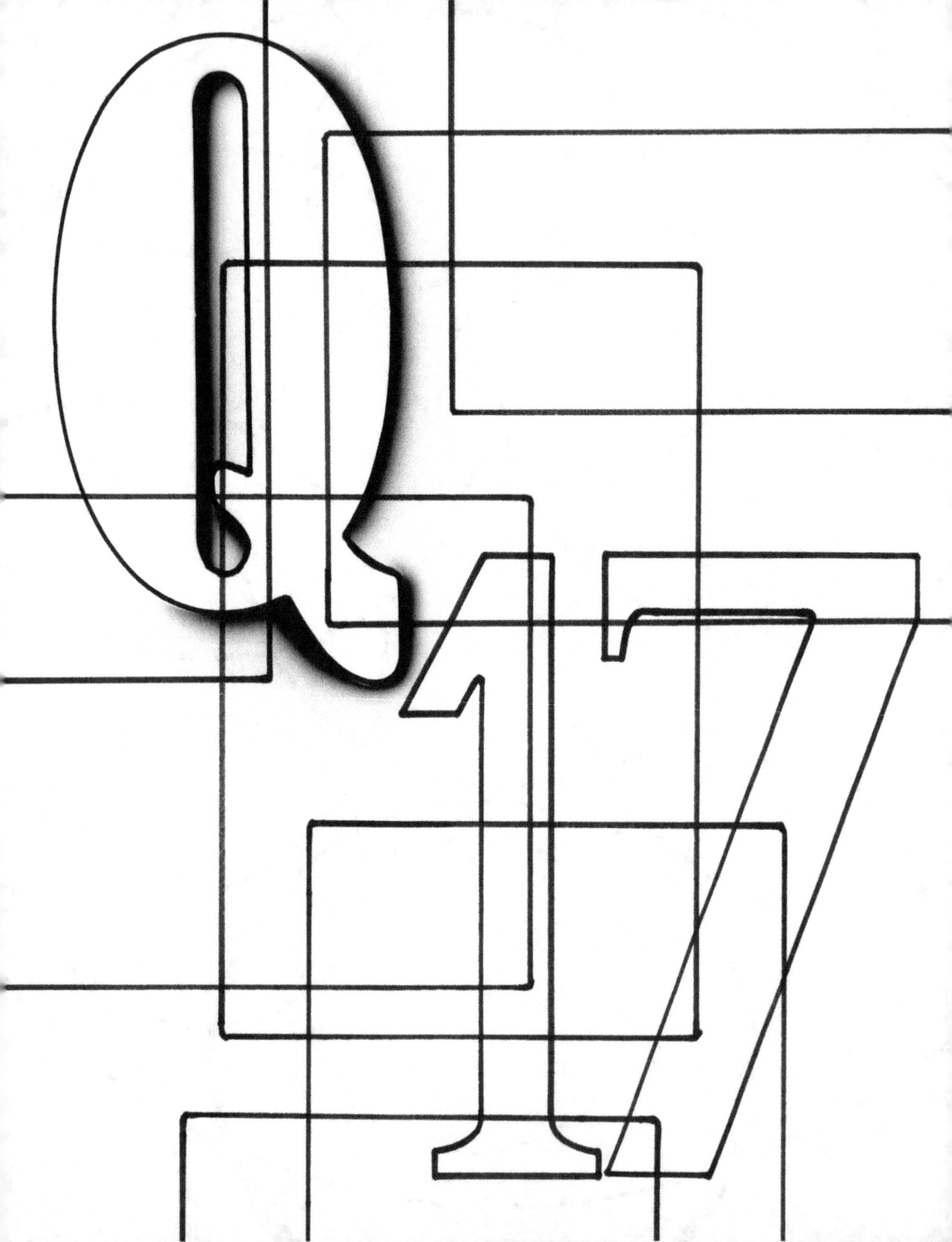

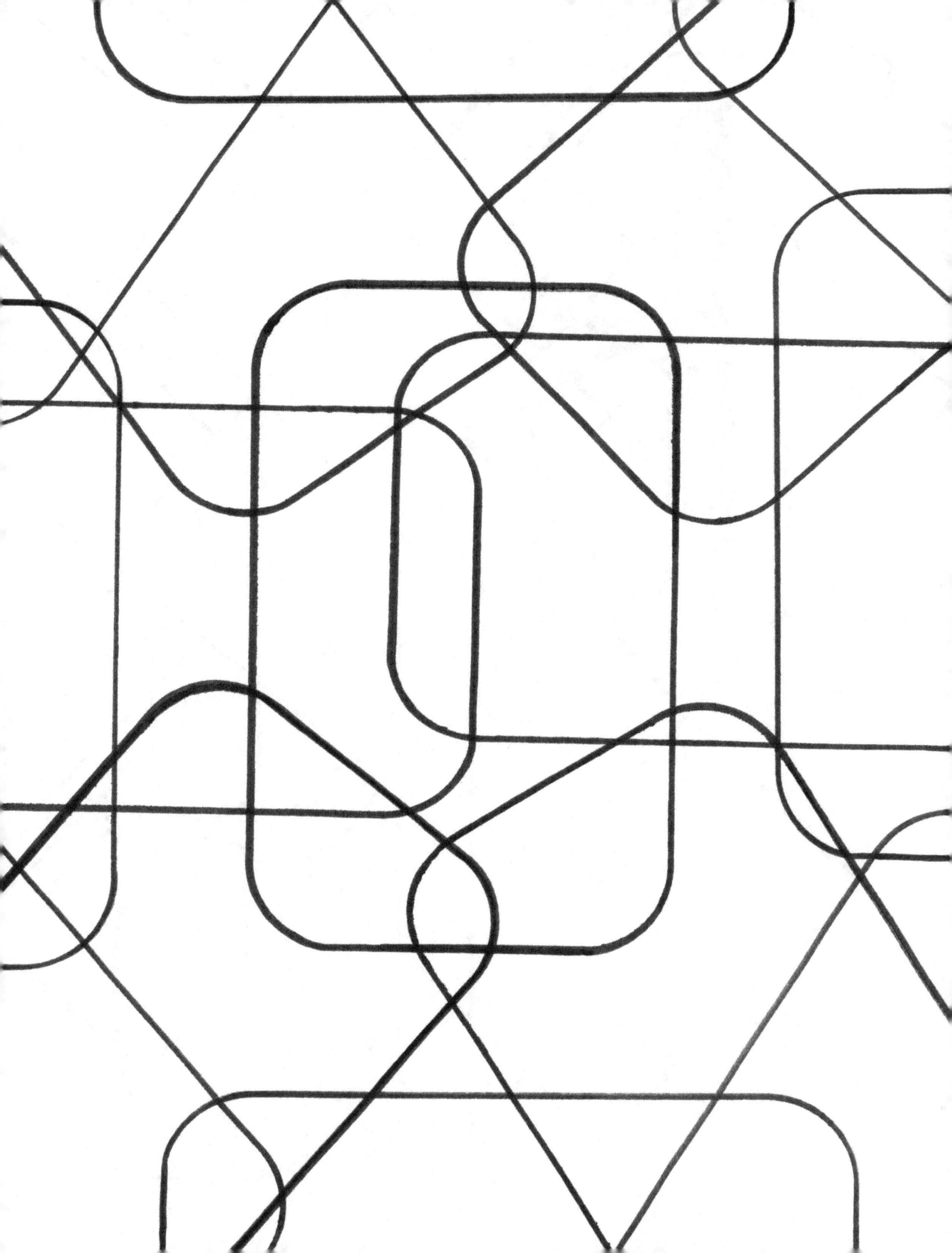

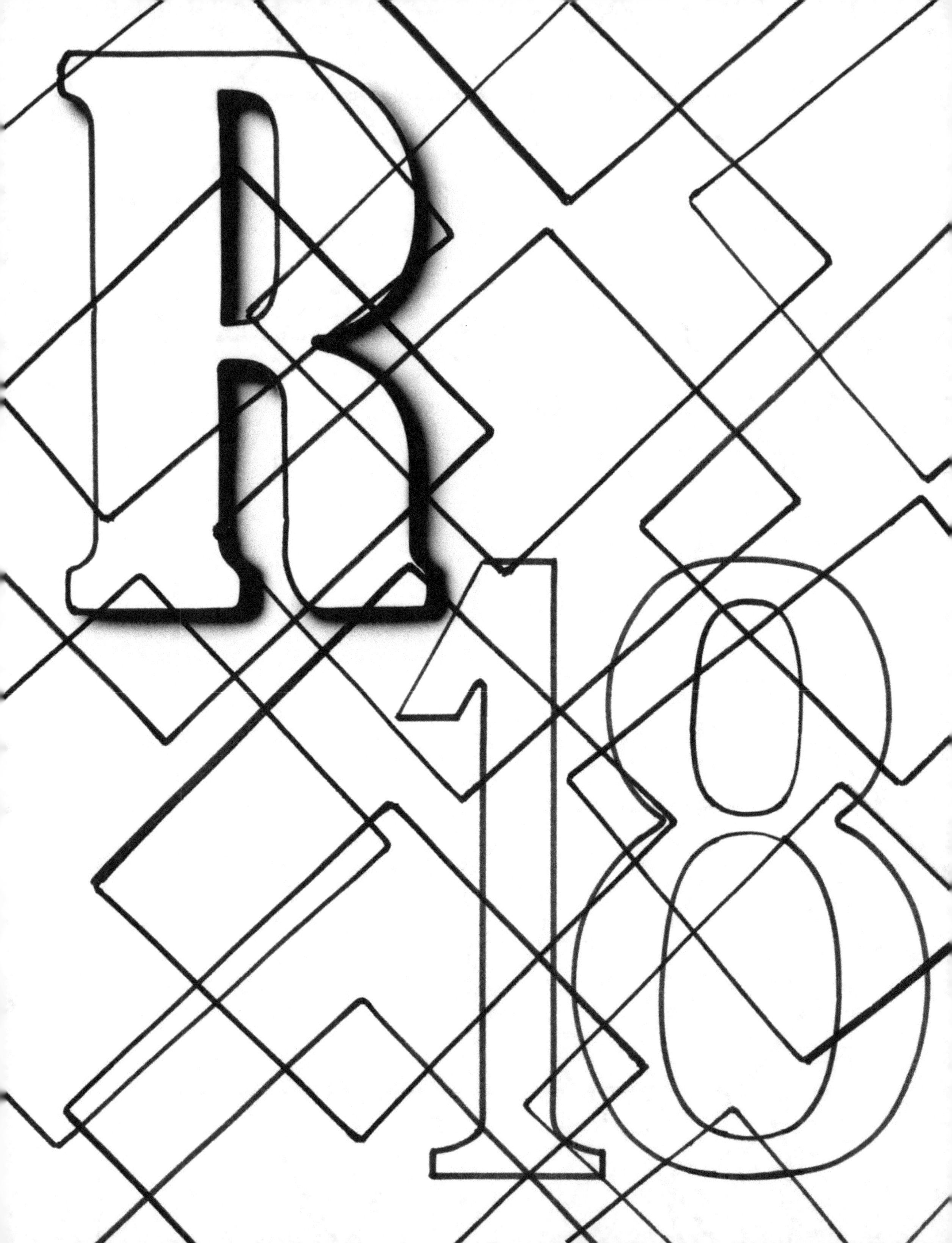

R18

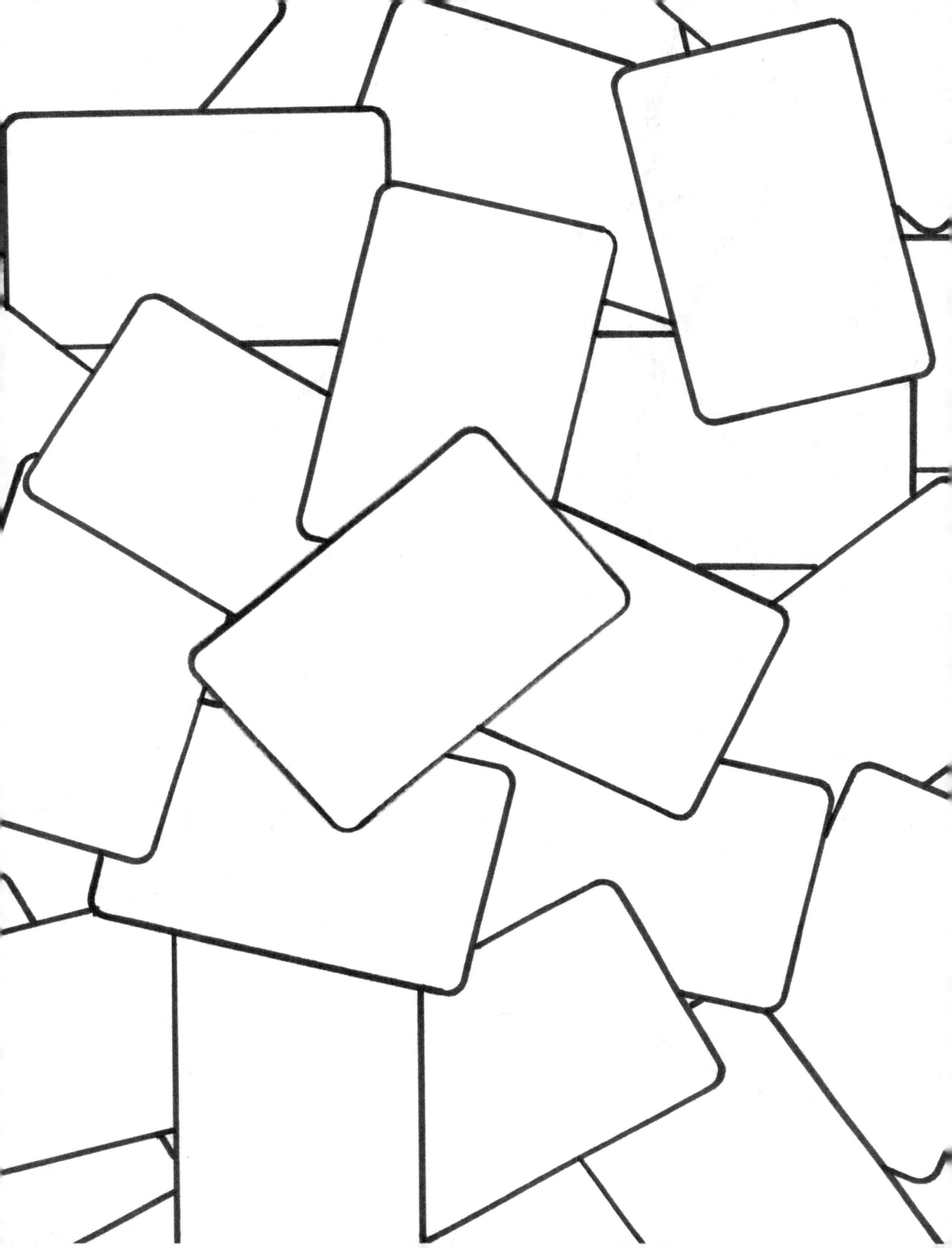

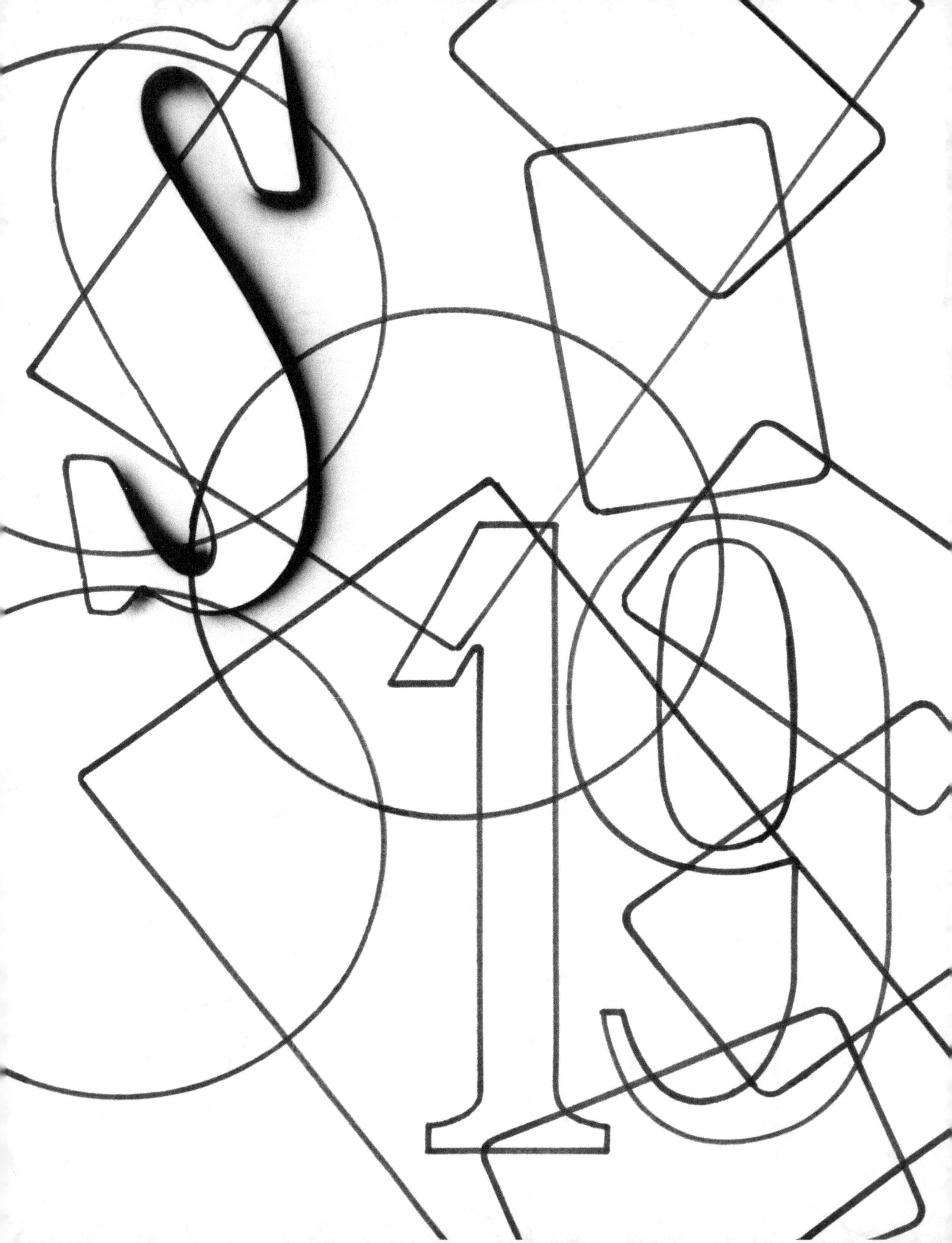

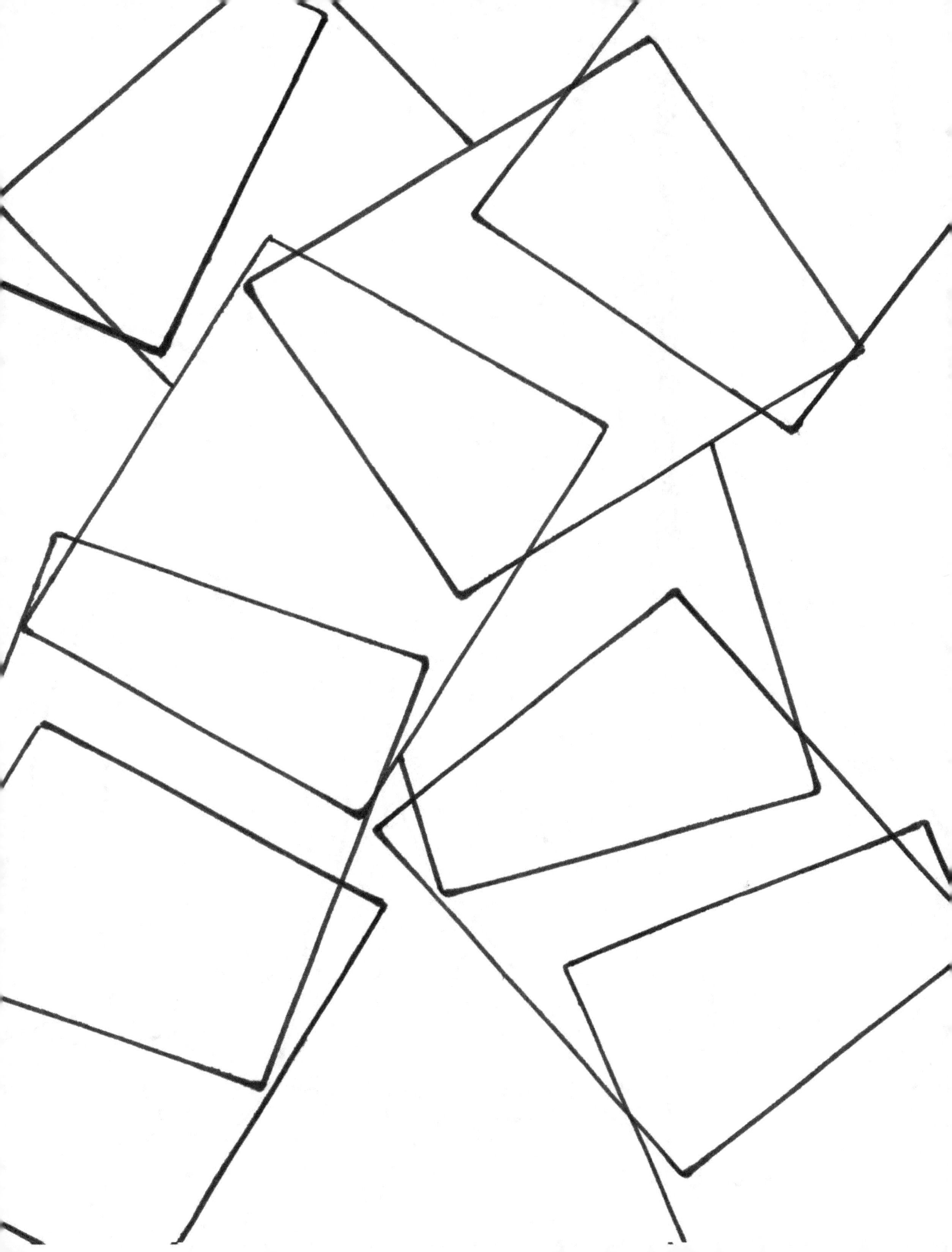

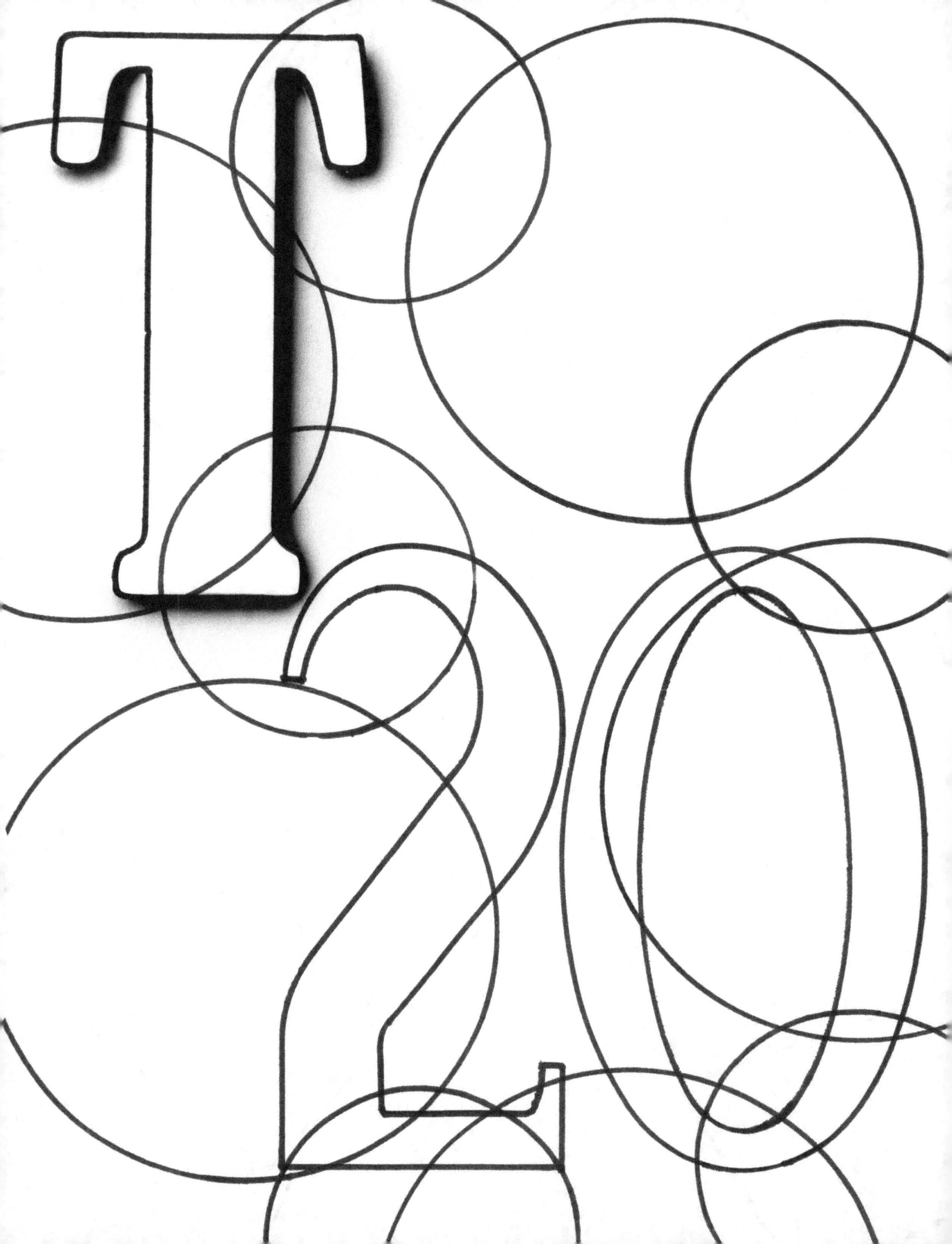

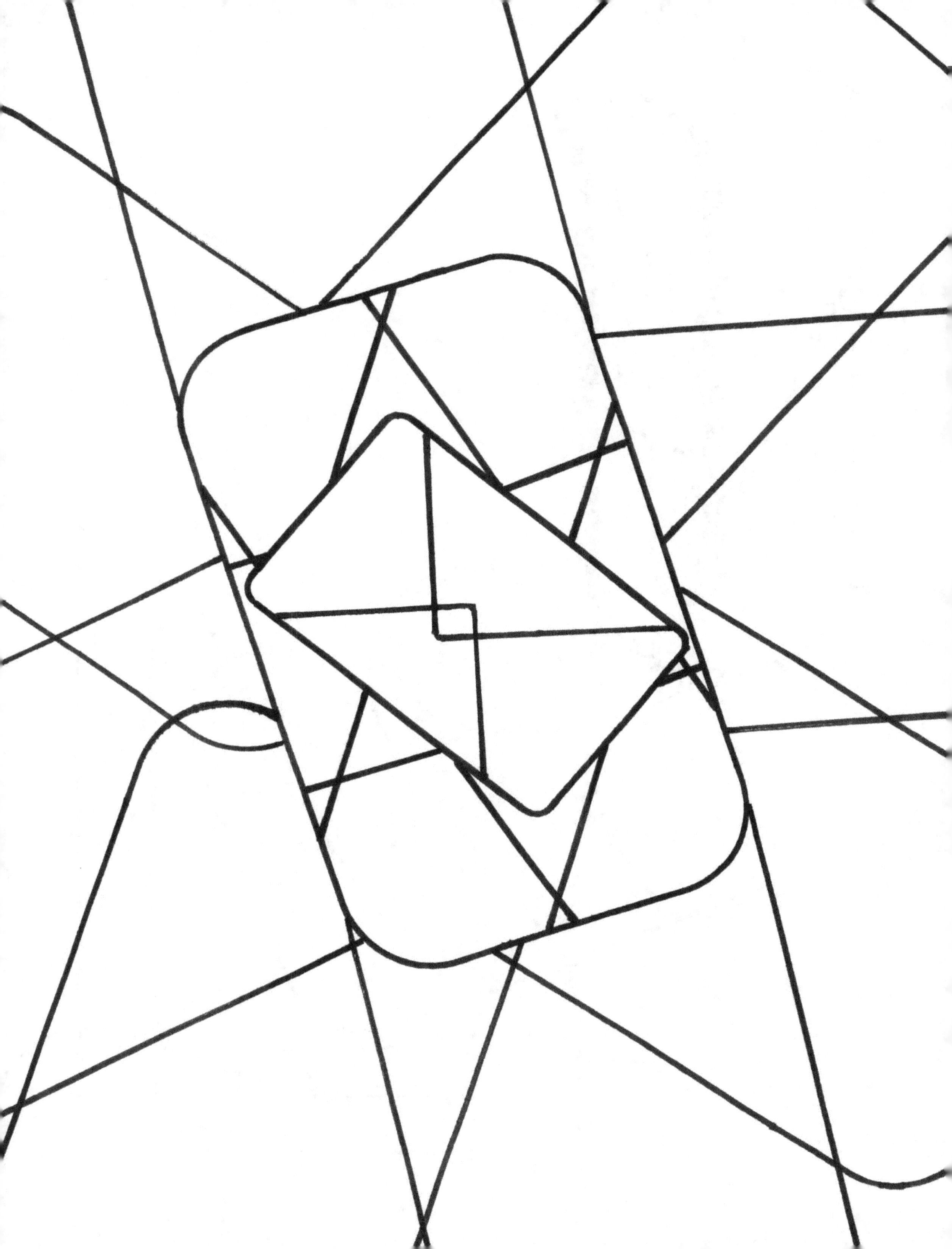

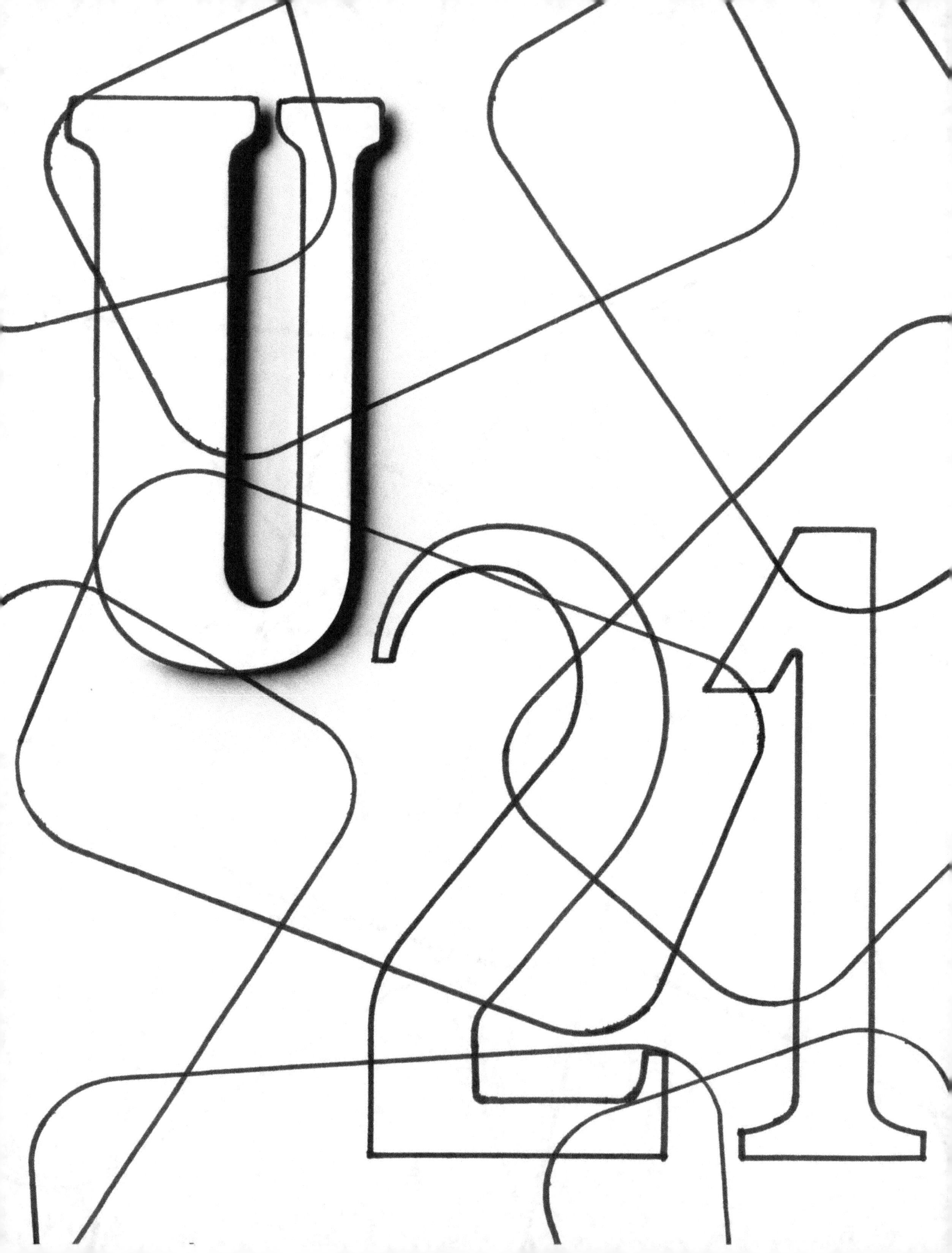

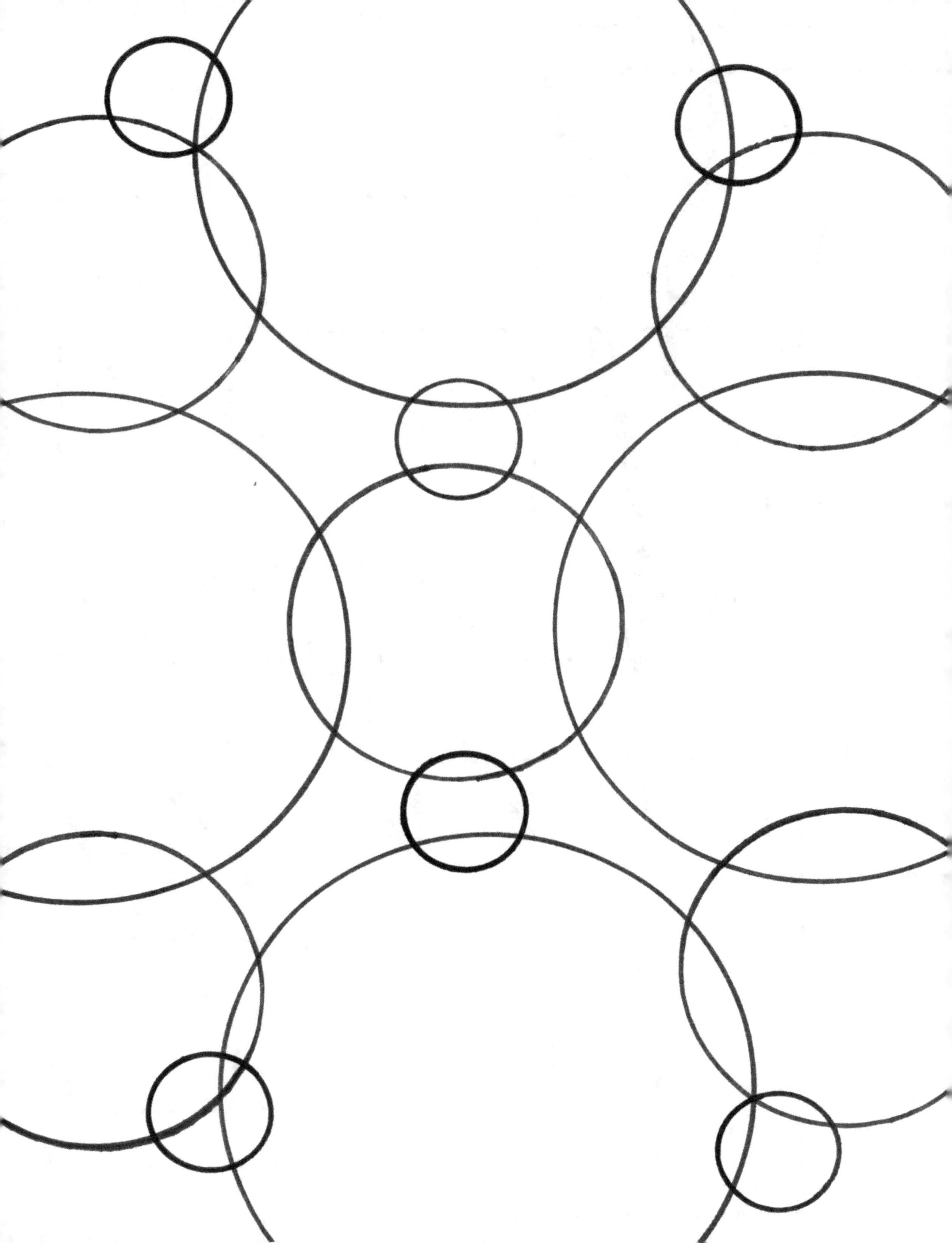

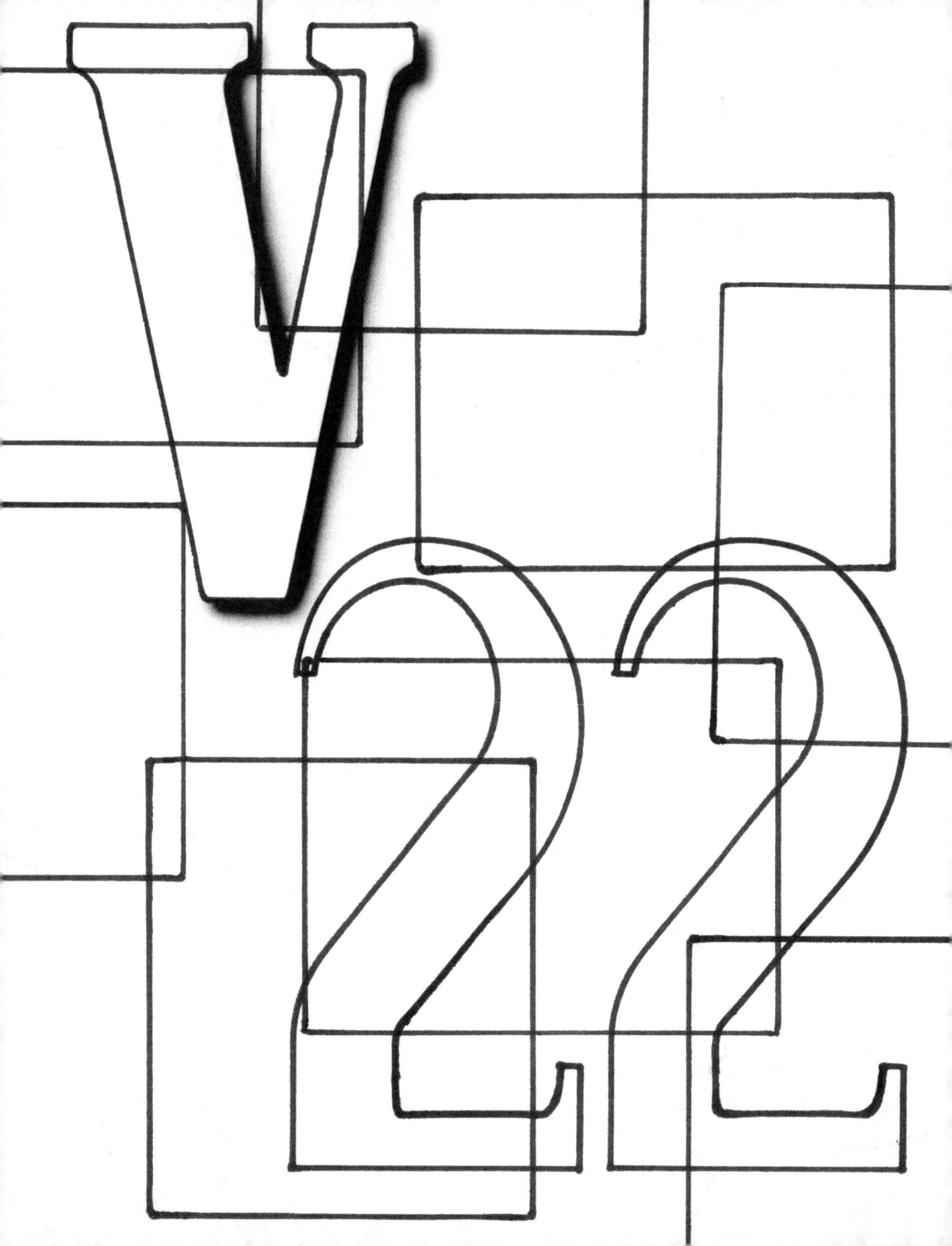

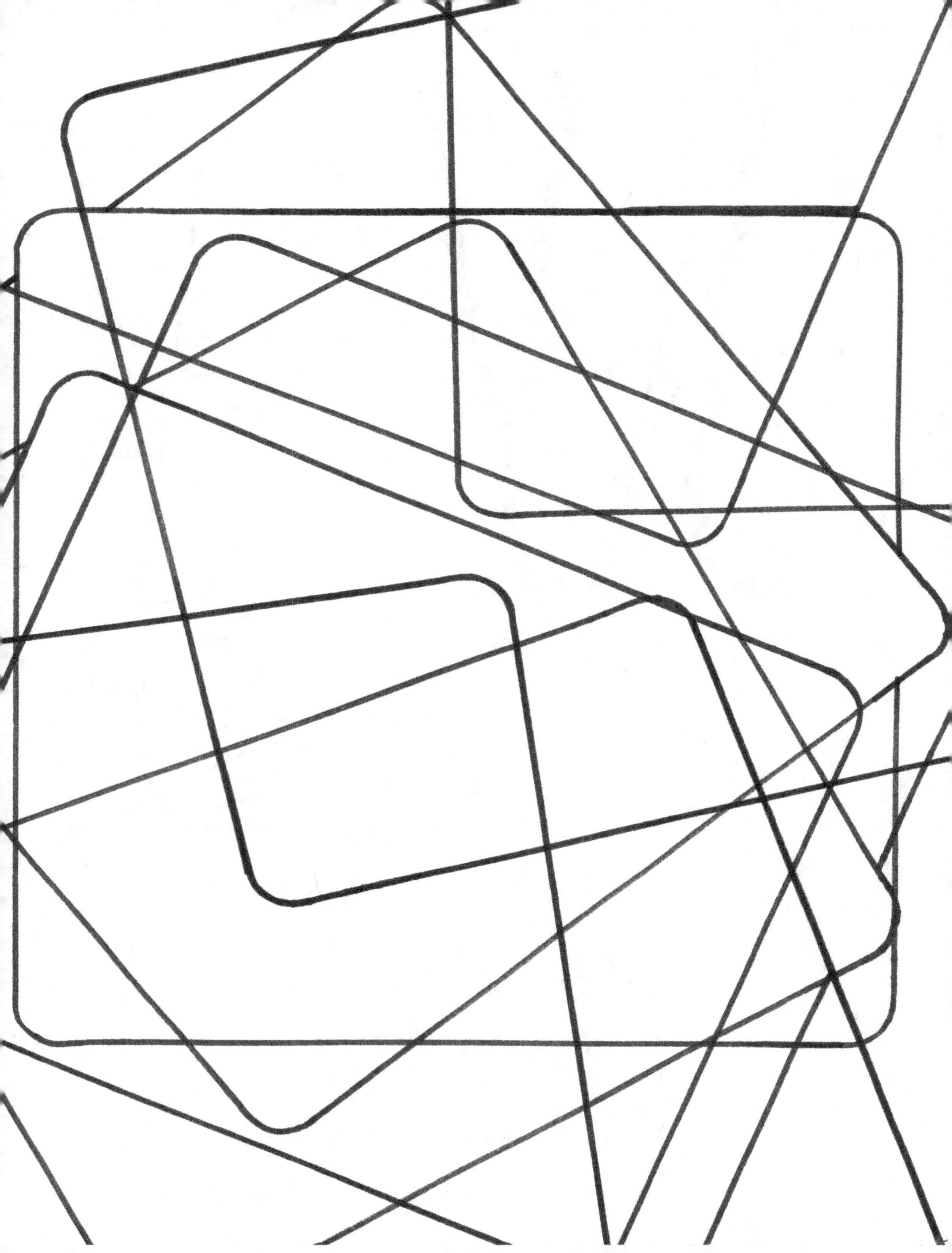

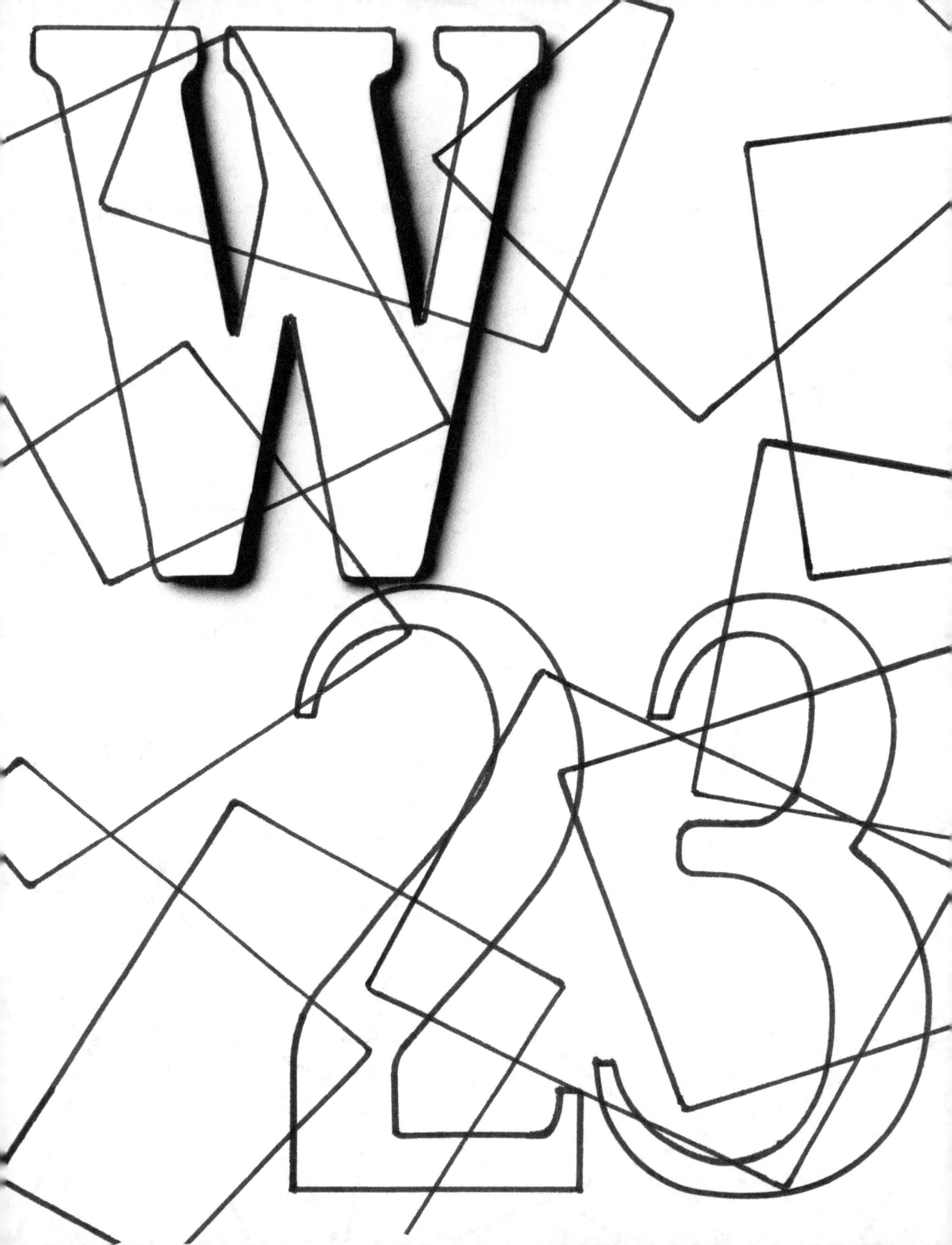

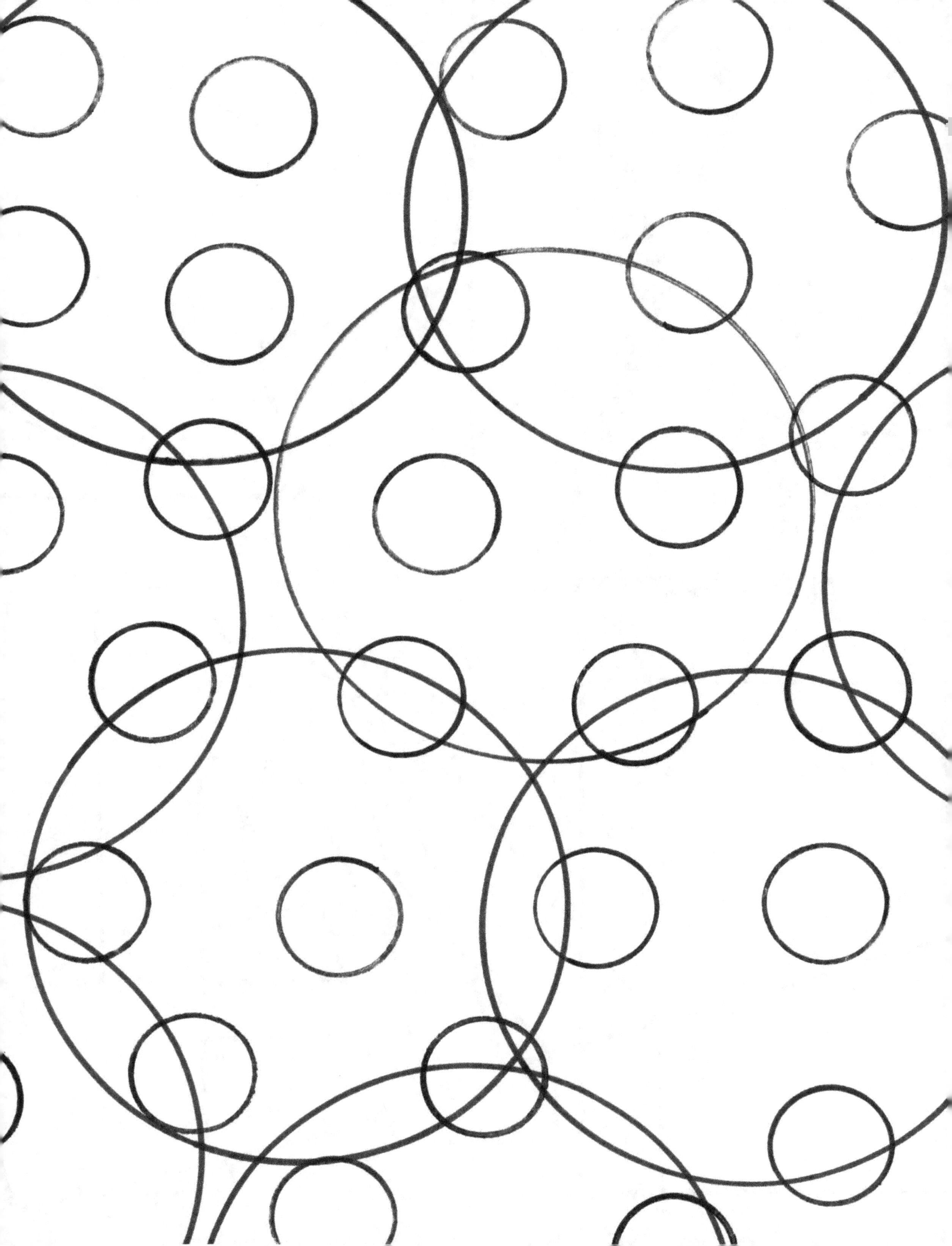

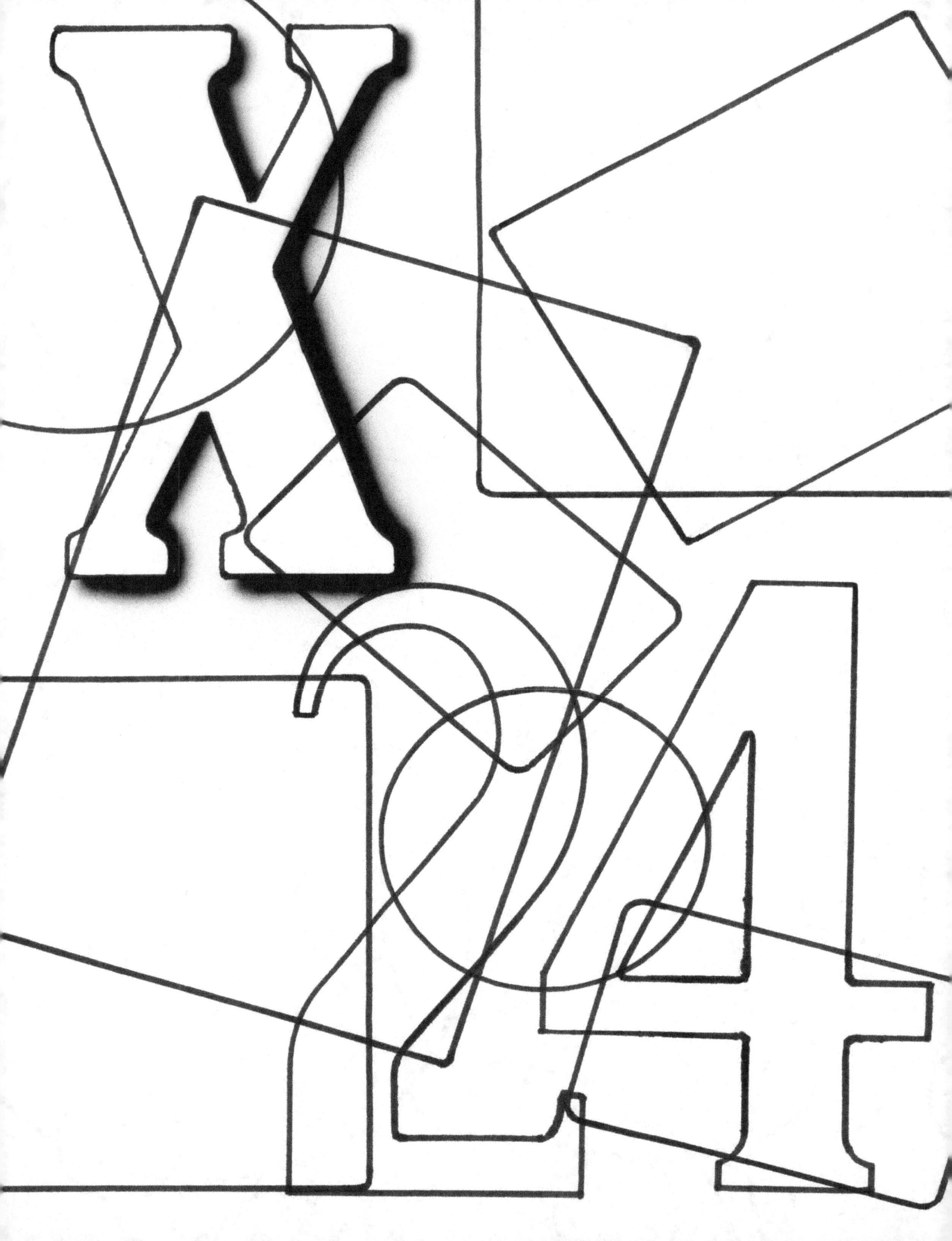

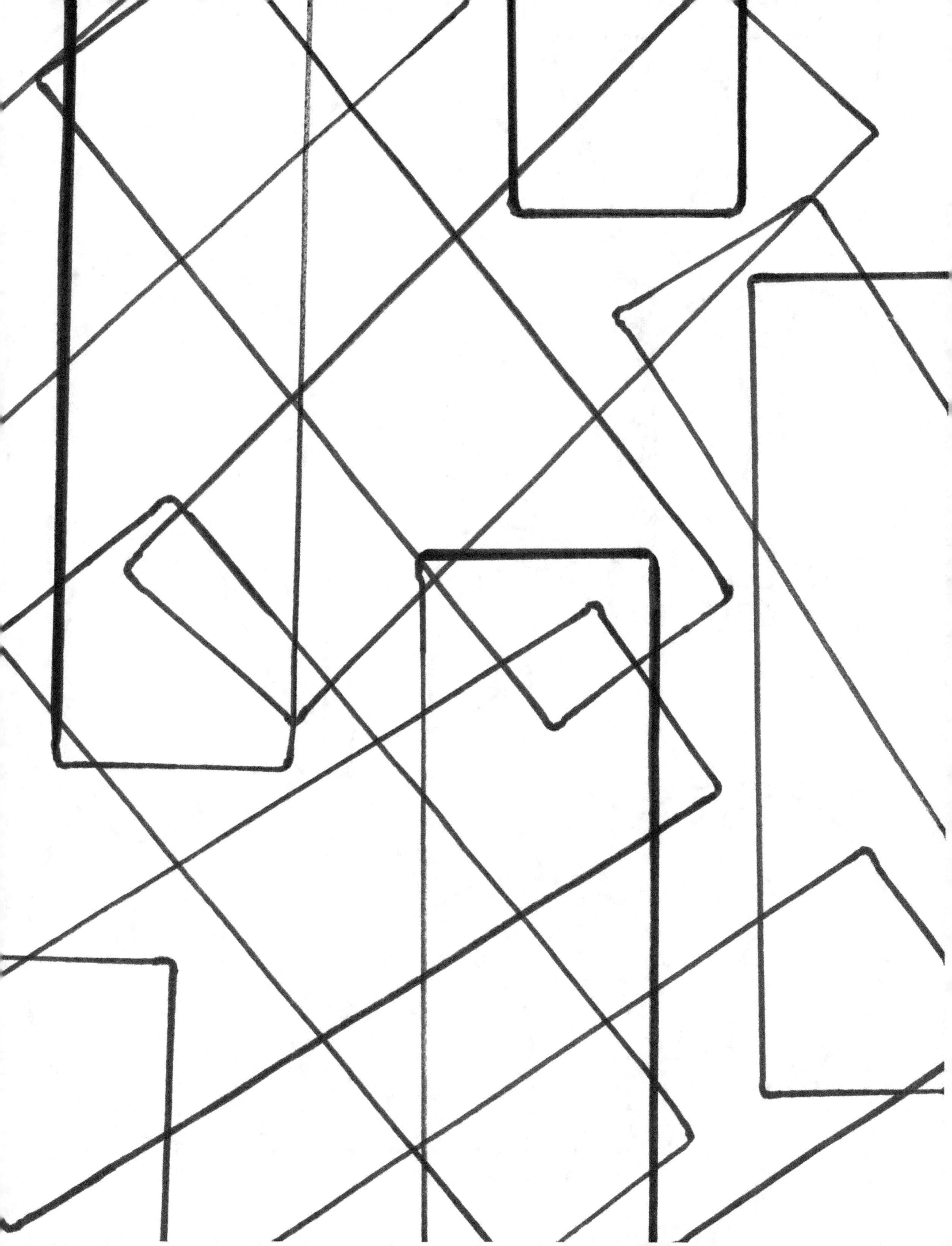

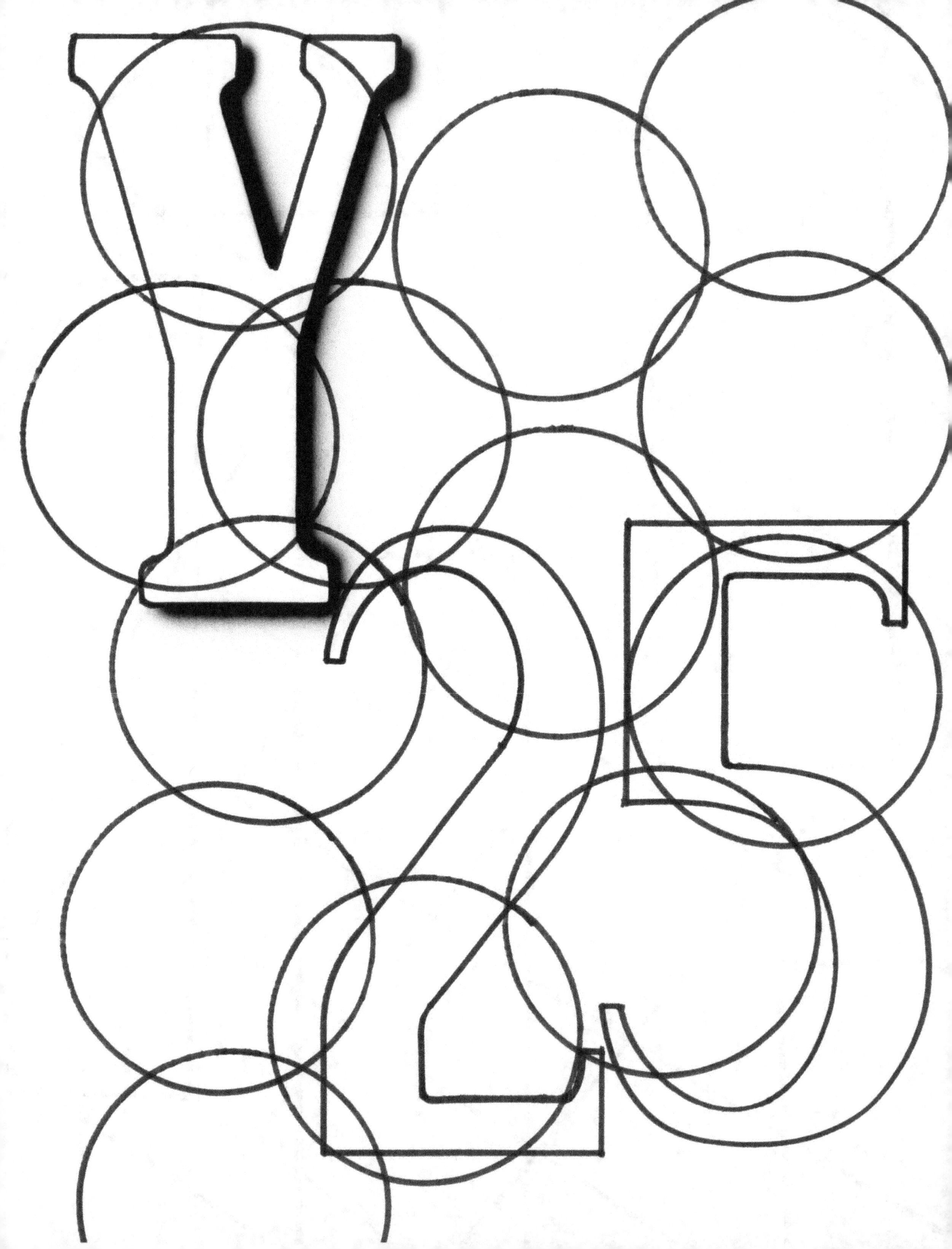

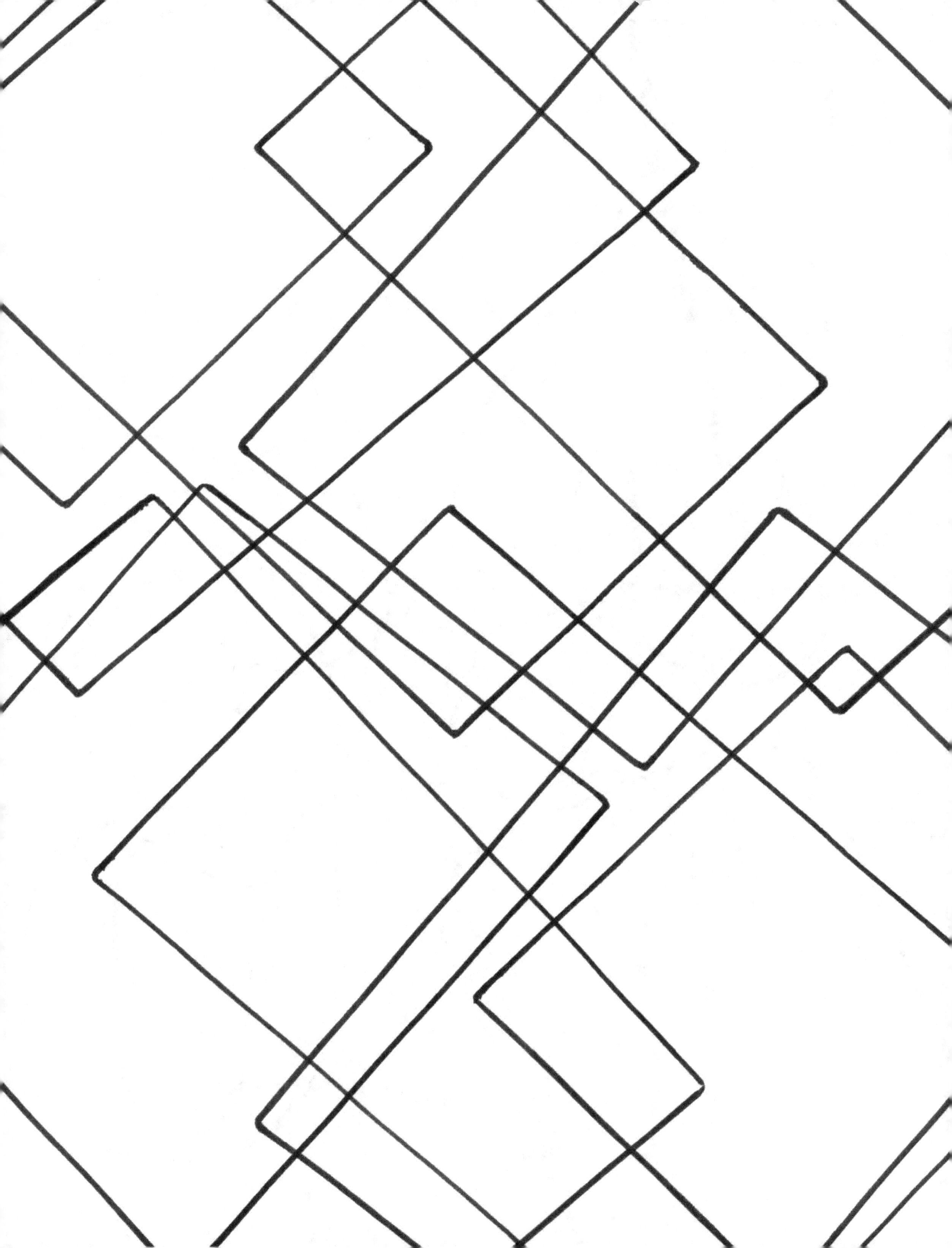

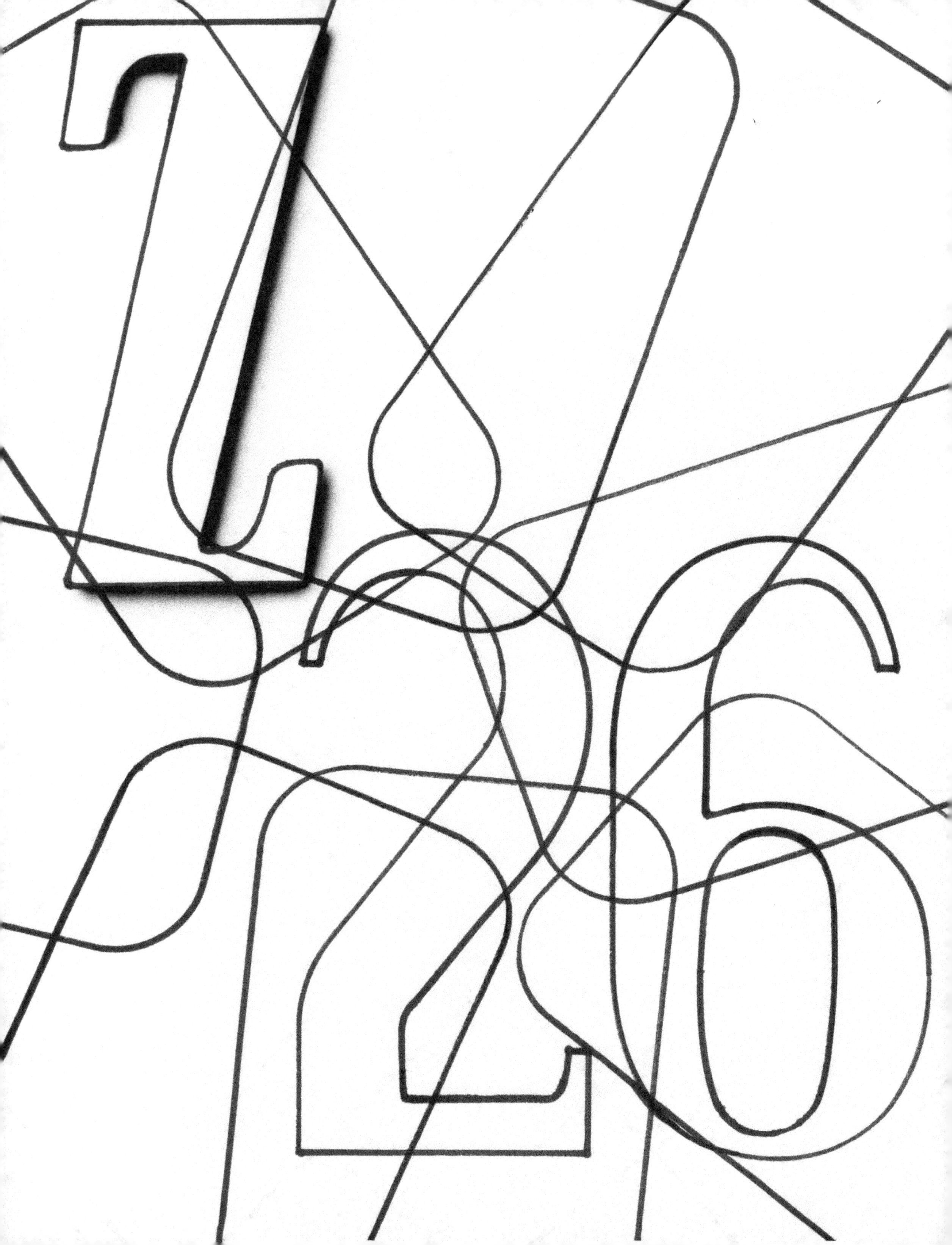

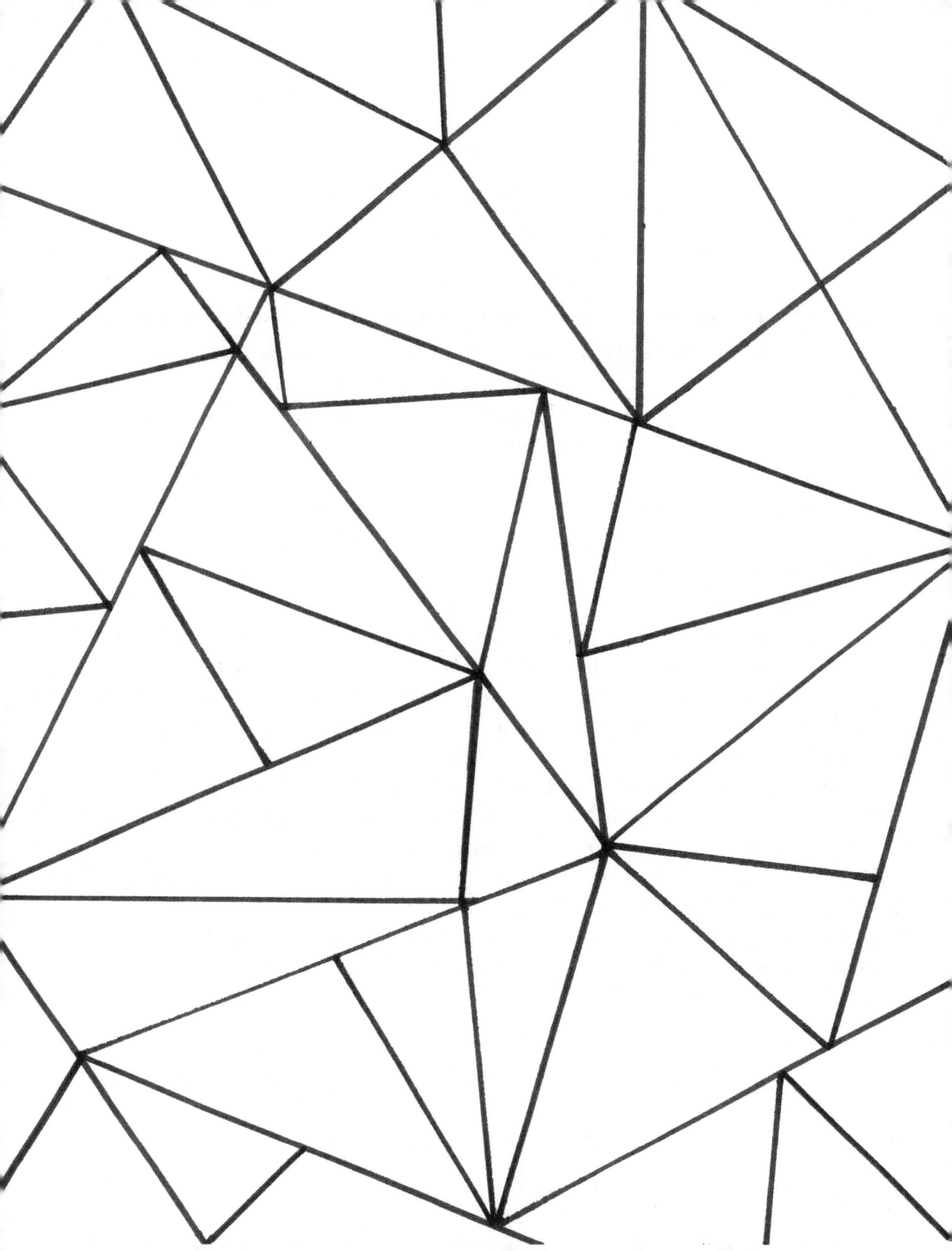

ACKNOWLEDGMENTS

I would like to give a special thanks to my wife Tammy of 26 yrs, for all your loving support.

A special acknowledgment to my children: Xavier, Kamon, Brielle &Abebe; always put
Jehovah God and His son Christ Jesus first and all things are possible.
"Dream It, Think It, Be It"
In loving memory of my mother Arlean S. Allen; she always gave me love and a smile,
encouraging me to do my best.

Special thanks to parents; Charles and Faye Allen; Marvin and Vervela Harris
(Do you like people today?) For your loving support.
Can not forget my brothers; Tony, Gordon, Mike, Markel and my sisters Zephrea, Jessica,
Tonya, Michelle and to lil sis in Tennessee. Love to you all, always.
A thanks to my uncles and aunts- James, Jimmy and Sunny; Shirley, Barbara, Teen and Ree;
Thank you for believing in me. (remember you bought my very 1st t-shirts)
Thanks to Howard and Peggy Gibbs for purchasing my very 1st original canvas painting.
To all my cousins(too many to name) thank you for your love and support- love you all.
To my brother in ART? DH2- Donald Hillsman ll, You Got SKILLZ!!!
To my sister Lady Money- Marlese Harris...The Hustle is Real and continues....
To Reggie and Barry from the "D", you 2 helped me take my craft (art) to the next level !!
Donald Hillsman Sr.,thanks for words you once told me "It Is What It Is"
To Gia'na Garel, the Coldest to pick up a pen and paint a masterpiece with words.
I'm glad "I Really Know You"
To Barbara G Middlebrooks, I know what it means to truly have a friend that I can depend on,
I really appreciate you helping me get this done, What's Next?

ABOUT THE AUTHOR

As an artist and entrepreneur of art for almost 35 years, Benjamin Allen takes a specialized, never-before-used process of blending plaster and paint, and creating pieces that offer the soul-stirring 3D effect of coming alive. As a sought after portrait painter, Allen has been commissioned for murals, as a faux finisher, and as a consultant on art related community projects. Acclaimed for his celebrity portraits, Allen has been commissioned by major stars to render their art. In addition to a partnership with Atlanta Designer Sharon Mann, of Sharon Mann Designs, he does faux finishes and painted galaxies across home theater ceilings throughout the region.

Recent clients have included the Tupac Shakur Museum, R&B legend Ronald Isley, The Isley Brothers, Russell Athletics, and murals featured on BRAVO Chnls seasons 1&2 -Married to Medicine; featuring a new Lego superhero mural in Mrs. Toya's son's room.

Allen's art has begun to adorned everything from motorcycles and car tags to bedroom murals, painted marbleized columns and custom painted rooms in show homes, super-sized canvases, and now various sundries and even a clothing/ T-shirt line officially launching in 2017, more at Portraitsthatbreathe.com